# Collins
### English for Exams

# Vocabulary
# for IELTS

Anneli Williams

HarperCollins Publishers
77-85 Fulham Palace Road
Hammersmith
London W6 8JB

First edition 2012

Reprint 10 9 8 7 6 5 4 3 2 1 0

© HarperCollins Publishers 2012

ISBN 978-0-00-745682-6

Collins ® is a registered trademark
of HarperCollins Publishers Limited

www.collinselt.com

A catalogue record for this book is available
from the British Library

Typeset in India by Aptara

Printed in Italy by LEGO SpA, Lavis (Trento)

# Contents

# Introduction

## Who is this book for?

*Vocabulary for IELTS* helps you improve your vocabulary when preparing for the IELTS examination. You can use the book to study on your own or as supplementary material for IELTS preparation classes. It is suitable for learners at level 5.0 to 5.5 aiming for band score 6.0 or higher.

## Summary

The *Vocabulary for IELTS* book and CD cover vocabulary items and skills which are relevant to all four exam papers: Listening, Reading, Writing and Speaking. In each unit, you work towards an exam practice exercise which is modelled on the actual IELTS exam. Each unit contains activities that help you develop, step-by-step, the vocabulary knowledge and skills to help you tackle the exam. Exam tips throughout the book highlight essential vocabulary-related learning strategies and exam techniques.

## Content
### Units

Each unit is divided into three parts.

**Part 1: Vocabulary** introduces vocabulary related to the topic or function of the unit. Definitions for this vocabulary are presented using Collins COBUILD full-sentence definitions, and IELTS-style example sentences show how the words are used in context. Parts of speech and the different forms of the words are also listed.

**Part 2: Practice exercises** provide a structured set of exercises which help you develop the skills to successfully apply vocabulary knowledge to the exam. Each unit focuses on developing vocabulary and skills for a particular paper, and the practice exercises provide practice for the particular paper.

**Part 3: Exam practice** provides exam practice exercises in a format that follows the actual exam giving you the opportunity to familiarize yourself with the kinds of questions you will encounter in the exam. This section focuses on a particular exam paper and is highlighted in grey for easy reference.

### Exam tips

There are exam tips and strategies in each unit. These are in boxes for easy reference.

### Audio script

All audio for the Listening and Speaking paper has been recorded on the CD using native speakers of English. A full audio script is provided at the back of the book so that you can check the language used in the listening and speaking exercises, if needed.

### Answer key

A comprehensive answer key is provided for all sections of the book including model answers for more open-ended writing and speaking tasks.

### Collocations

At the back of the book, you can further develop your vocabulary by studying the list of the most common collocations for the vocabulary presented in the units.

# How to use this book

The book is divided into 20 units. <u>Units 1-9 cover vocabulary</u> for topics that frequently appear in the exam, such as health and education. <u>Units 11-19 cover words for general functions</u>, such as describing problems and solutions. Units 10 and 20 provide revision exercises. Unit 10 revises the vocabulary and skills covered in Units 1-9, and Unit 20 revises the vocabulary and skills covered in Units 11-19. All 20 units help you develop skills such as paraphrasing and working out the meaning of unfamiliar words from context.

Each unit is self-contained so that you can study the units in any order. You can choose the unit you want to study either by selecting the topic you want to study, or by selecting which exam paper you want to practise. Only the units with practice on the Speaking and Listening papers contain audio. The contents pages at the beginning of the book provide an overview of what is in each unit so you can use this to choose which units you would like to study first. These pages also give you information on which units contain audio.

You will probably find it helpful to begin each unit by reading the vocabulary items in part 1, then working through the exercises in preparation for the exam practice exercise at the end. Try to do the exam exercises within the time limit to give yourself realistic exam practice.

In order to learn a new word, it is usually necessary to revisit it several times. The revision units help you to do this. However, it is also a good idea to avoid writing your answers in the book so that you can do the exercises again at a later date.

It is also advisable to keep a vocabulary notebook. Knowing a word and how to use it involves understanding many aspects of it. The more information you can record about the words you are learning, the more useful it will be. Key definitions, part(s) of speech, common collocations and example sentences are all very helpful. Don't forget to use the Collocations section at the back of the book to help with this.

Getting well-informed feedback on your writing and speaking exam practice exercises would also be an advantage. However, if this is not possible it is still important to do the exercises in full. Studying model answers can help you develop the ability to assess your own work. If possible, record yourself when speaking, and listen carefully to your performance. Avoid memorising model answers. Remember that in the actual exam, it is important to answer the question and not just speak or write about the topic

As a final preparation before the exam, you could re-read the exam tips in the boxes. This will remind you of the strategies for success in the exam.

# 1 People and relationships

## Vocabulary

### People in relationship:

- **client (clients)**
  - NOUN A **client** of a professional person or organization is a person that receives a service from them in return for payment. ▪ *a solicitor and his client* ▪ *The company requires clients to pay substantial fees in advance.*
- **colleague (colleagues)**
  - NOUN Your **colleagues** are the people you work with, especially in a professional job. ▪ *Female academics are still paid less than their male colleagues.* ▪ *In the corporate world, the best sources of business are your former colleagues.*
- **employer (employers)**
  - NOUN Your **employer** is the person or organization that you work for. ▪ *employers who hire illegal workers* ▪ *The telephone company is the country's largest employer.*
- **parent (parents)**
  - NOUN Your **parents** are your mother and father. ▪ *Children need their parents.* ▪ *When you become a parent the things you once cared about seem to have less value.*
- **sibling (siblings)**
  - NOUN Your **siblings** are your brothers and sisters. [FORMAL] ▪ *Some studies have found that children are more friendly to younger siblings of the same sex.* ▪ *Sibling rivalry often causes parents anxieties.*
- **spouse (spouses)**
  - NOUN Someone's **spouse** is the person they are married to. *Husbands and wives do not have to pay any inheritance tax when their spouse dies.*

### Describing people:

- **autonomous**
  - ADJECTIVE An **autonomous person** makes their own decisions rather than being influenced by someone else ▪ *They proudly declared themselves part of a new autonomous province.* ▪ *the liberal idea of the autonomous individual*
- **consistent**
  - ADJECTIVE Someone who is **consistent** always behaves in the same way, has the same attitudes towards people or things, or achieves the same level of success in something. ▪ *Becker has never been the most consistent of players anyway.* ▪ *his consistent support of free trade* ▪ *a consistent character with a major thematic function*
- **conventional**
  - ADJECTIVE Someone who is **conventional** has behaviour and opinions that are ordinary and normal. ▪ *a respectable married woman with conventional opinions* ▪ *this close, fairly conventional English family*
- **co-operative** also **cooperative**
  - ADJECTIVE If you say that someone is **co-operative**, you mean that they do what you ask them without complaining or arguing. ▪ *The president said the visit would develop friendly and co-operative relations between the two countries.* ▪ *a contented and co-operative workforce*
- **efficient**
  - ADJECTIVE If something or someone is **efficient**, they are able to do tasks

successfully, without wasting time or energy. ▪ *With today's more efficient contraception women can plan their families and careers.* ▪ *Technological advances allow more efficient use of labour.* ▪ *an efficient way of testing thousands of compounds*

- **flexible**
ADJECTIVE Something or someone that is **flexible** is able to change easily and adapt to different conditions and circumstances. ▪ *more flexible arrangements to allow access to services after normal working hours* ▪ *We encourage flexible working.*

- **idealistic**
ADJECTIVE If you describe someone as **idealistic**, you mean that they have ideals, and base their behaviour on these ideals, even if this may be impractical. ▪ *Idealistic young people died for the cause.* ▪ *an over-simplistic and idealistic vision of family dynamics*

- **tolerant**
ADJECTIVE If you describe someone as **tolerant**, you approve of the fact that they allow other people to say and do as they like, even if they do not agree with or like it. ▪ [+*of*] *They need to be tolerant of different points of view.* ▪ *Other changes include more tolerant attitudes to unmarried couples having children.*

- **vulnerable**
ADJECTIVE Someone who is **vulnerable** is weak and without protection, with the result that they are easily hurt physically or emotionally. ▪ *Old people are particularly vulnerable members of our society.*

## Practice exercises

**1**  Circle the words that you associate with family relationships. Underline the words you associate with professional relationships.

| | | | |
|---|---|---|---|
| **a** | client | **d** | colleague |
| **b** | parent | **e** | spouse |
| **c** | sibling | **f** | employer |

**2**  Listen to three speakers talking about people who have been important to them. Indicate the person each speaker describes by writing a letter a–f from Exercise 1 in each space.

01

1 _____

2 _____

3 _____

### Exam tip:
- You can often recognize whether a word is a noun, verb, adjective or adverb from its ending.
- Adjectives can have many different endings, but these are common.

| -able/-ible | *vulnerable, flexible* | -ic | *idealistic* |
|---|---|---|---|
| -al | *conventional* | -ive | *co-operative* |
| -ant/-ent | *tolerant, consistent, efficient* | -ous | *autonomous* |

- Learn to recognize these.

🎧 **3** Listen again to the three speakers and write down the adjectives from the table above that you hear. Listen for the word endings: -able, -ible, -al, -ant, -ent, -ic, -ive, -ous.

**1** _____

**2** _____

**3** _____

> **Exam tip:** In Part 4 of the IELTS Listening exam you have to listen to a talk on a topic of general academic interest.
>
> You do not need to know all of the vocabulary.
>
> If you hear a word you don't know, listen for expressions like:
>
> **a** i.e.
> **b** in other words
> **c** that is
> **d** by ... I mean
> **e** that is to say
>
> The text that follows these expressions helps you understand the word.
>
> Example: *Employers value* **conscientious** *workers, that is workers who complete tasks with care.*

🎧 **4** Listen to the extract from a lecture about only children and notice the expression the speaker uses to indicate she is defining the key expressions 1–6 below. Look back at the Exam tip and write a letter a–e in each space.

**1** only children _____

**2** parental resources _____

**3** tolerant _____

**4** co-operative _____

**5** autonomy _____

**6** unconventional _____

🎧 **5** Listen to the extract again and complete the definitions the speaker gives for words 1–6 above. Write one word in each space.

**1** only children – 'children without _____.'

**2** parental resources – 'not just money, but also _____ and _____.'

**3** tolerant – 'able to accept _____.'

**4** co-operative – 'able to work _____ with _____.'

**5** autonomy – 'ability to _____ their own _____.'

**6** unconventional – 'not quite _____ in social terms'

# Exam practice: Listening exam Section 4

🎧
03

Listen to the lecture extract about birth order and personality and answer questions 1–5 by choosing the correct letter A, B or C.

> **Exam tip:** Listen for key adjectives and clues in the context for what they mean.

1   What does the speaker discuss in relation to personality?

   **A**  Family size

   **B**  The relationship between children and their parents

   **C**  People's position in the family

2   What does the speaker imply about anxiety?

   **A**  It is a positive trait.

   **B**  It is a negative trait.

   **C**  It is experienced by younger siblings.

3   What do some researchers say about youngest children?

   **A**  They form relationships easily.

   **B**  They agree with the opinions of other people.

   **C**  They like it if people agree with them.

4   Why are middle children considered to be rebellious?

   **A**  They don't like to be told what to do.

   **B**  They don't know how to be agreeable.

   **C**  They like to be different from others.

5   What does the speaker say about the quality of research on birth order?

   **A**  Most research has been done correctly.

   **B**  Most research has been done incorrectly.

   **C**  Most research has come to a clear conclusion.

# 2 Health

## Vocabulary

### Health problems:

- **addiction (addictions)**
  NOUN **Addiction** is the condition of taking harmful drugs and being unable to stop taking them. ▪ *long-term addiction to nicotine*

- **allergy (allergies)**
  NOUN If you have a particular **allergy**, you become ill or get a rash when you eat, smell, or touch something that does not normally make people ill. ▪ *Food allergies can result in an enormous variety of different symptoms.*

- **cancer (cancers)**
  NOUN **Cancer** is a serious disease in which cells in a person's body increase rapidly in an uncontrolled way, producing abnormal growths. ▪ *a cancer research charity*

- **dehydration**
  UNCOUNTABLE NOUN You are suffering from **dehydration** if you lose too much water from your body. ▪ *Cholera causes severe dehydration.*

- **disease (diseases)**
  NOUN A **disease** is an illness that affects people, animals or plants, for example one which is caused by bacteria or infection.
  ▪ *the rapid spread of disease in the area*

- **infection (infections)**
  NOUN An **infection** is a disease caused by germs or bacteria. ▪ *Ear infections are common in pre-school children.*

- **obesity**
  UNCOUNTABLE NOUN Someone suffering from **obesity** is extremely fat. ▪ *The excessive consumption of sugar leads to obesity.*

- **stroke (strokes)**
  NOUN If someone has a **stroke**, a blood vessel in their brain bursts or becomes blocked, which may kill them or make them unable to move one side of their body. ▪ *He had a minor stroke in 1987, which left him partly paralyzed.*

### Verbs associated with treatment:

- **administer (administers, administering, administered)**
  VERB If a doctor or nurse **administers** a drug, they give it to a patient. ▪ *Paramedics are trained to administer certain drugs.*

- **admit (admits, admitting, admitted)**
  VERB If someone is **admitted** to hospital they are taken into hospital for treatment and kept there until they are well enough to go home. ▪ *She was admitted to hospital with a soaring temperature.*

- **diagnose (diagnoses, diagnosing, diagnosed)** / diagnose with / as having
  VERB If someone or something **is diagnosed as** having a particular illness or problem, their illness or problem is identified.
  ▪ *Almost a million people are diagnosed with colon cancer each year.*

- **discharge (discharges, discharging, discharged)**
  VERB When someone is **discharged from** hospital, they are officially allowed to leave, or told they must leave. ▪ *He has a broken nose but may be discharged today.*

- **examine (examines, examining, examined)**
  VERB If a doctor **examines** you, he or she looks at your body, feels it, or does simple

tests in order to check how healthy you are. ▪ *Another doctor examined her and could still find nothing wrong.*

- **screen (screens, screening, screened)** VERB To **screen for** a disease means to examine people to make sure that they do not have it. ▪ *Men over 50 are routinely screened for prostate abnormalities.*

- **vaccinate (vaccinates, vaccinating, vaccinated)** VERB A vaccine is a harmless form of the germs that cause a particular disease. If a person or animal **is vaccinated**, they are given a vaccine, usually by injection, to prevent them getting that disease. ▪ *Dogs must be vaccinated against distemper.*

## Practice exercises

1  The words below describe different disorders. Circle the words that you associate with rich countries. Underline the words you associate with poor countries.

| | | | |
|---|---|---|---|
| **a** | infection | **e** | stroke |
| **b** | heart disease | **f** | dehydration |
| **c** | allergies | **g** | addiction |
| **d** | obesity | | |

2  Read the passage below and compare your answers to Exercise 1 with the information in the passage.  *wealth*

### Diseases of Affluence – Diseases of Poverty

Health conditions associated with wealth are sometimes referred to as diseases of affluence. These include diseases which are not communicable, such as Type 2 diabetes, cancer, and stroke as well as alcohol and drug addiction, obesity and some allergies. Risk factors for these conditions are associated with the lifestyle of the economically prosperous, in particular: physical inactivity, easy availability of meat, sugar, salt and processed foods, excessive consumption of alcohol and tobacco, and lower exposure to infectious agents.

The diseases of poverty, in contrast, are predominantly infectious diseases such as HIV/AIDS, tuberculosis, malaria and diarrhoeal diseases. Risk factors for these conditions include: overcrowding, inadequate sanitation, malnutrition, and inadequate access to health care. Millions of lives could be saved every year by addressing these underlying problems and by simple preventive measures such as immunizing the population against common infectious agents.

> **Exam tip:** In the IELTS Reading exam you may have to indicate whether statements about a passage are True, False or Not given (i.e. not mentioned).
>
> You can often recognize a True statement if you can match it to a part of the passage that expresses the same idea in different words.
>
> Recognizing synonyms (words with approximately the same meaning) can help you do this.
>
> Example: *Allergies are common in* **wealthy** *countries. Allergies are common in* **affluent** *countries.*

**3** Underline words in the passage for Exercise 2 which could be replaced by the words in bold below.

**1** Minor skin **disorders** do not normally require hospital treatment.

**2** **Misuse** of prescription drugs is a growing problem.

**3** **Germs** can cause stomach upsets.

**4** **Vaccinating** children against measles has reduced the prevalence of this disease.

**4** The words below describe actions that medical staff may take when a person enters hospital. Number the verbs from 1 to 5 to show the order in which they typically occur.

| diagnose ____ | discharge ____ | admit ____ | treat ____ | examine ____ |
|---|---|---|---|---|

> **Exam tip:** In the IELTS Reading exam you may have to complete gaps in sentences with words from a reading passage. Recognizing collocations (i.e. words that commonly go together) can help you do this.
>
> If you look carefully at the words on either side of the gap you may be able to use your knowledge of collocations to choose the right word(s).
>
> Example: *The patient was _____ for cancer. The patient was treated for cancer.*

**5** Complete the sentences below with words a–e. Look carefully at the prepositions after the gaps to help you choose the right word.

| **a** vaccinated | **b** diagnosed | **c** screened | **d** administered | **e** discharged |
|---|---|---|---|---|

**1** In poor countries patients are sometimes _____ from hospital before they are fully cured.

**2** If all women over the age of 50 are _____ for breast cancer, many lives can be saved.

**3** The patient was _____ with heart disease.

**4** All children should be _____ against infectious diseases such as measles.

**5** The doctor _____ a drug to the patient to help him sleep.

# Exam practice: Reading – answering True/False/ Not given questions – completing sentences

## QUESTIONS 1–4

*Do the statements 1–4 below agree with the information given in the following text? Write:*

| | |
|---|---|
| TRUE | *if the text confirms the statement* |
| FALSE | *if the text confirms the opposite of the statement* |
| NOT GIVEN | *if it is impossible to know from the text* |

**Tip:** Look for synonyms for key terms.

Scientists from the UK and USA have recently reported that over the last 30 years the incidence of Type 2 diabetes has more than doubled. They estimate that nearly 350 million adults worldwide now have the disease. In every country studied, rates of diabetes had either remained the same or increased. The rise has been particularly acute in the Pacific Islands with up to thirty per cent of women in some areas suffering from the condition.

Type 2 diabetes is a chronic progressive condition which occurs when there is too much glucose in the blood, either because the pancreas does not produce enough insulin or because cells have become resistant to insulin. Complications resulting from diabetes include damage to kidneys, blindness, heart disease and strokes.

The condition is associated with obesity; however, nearly three-quarters of the rise has been attributed to longer lifespans and better diagnosis. Having a close relative with the disease is also a risk factor.

Type 2 diabetes has also become a major burden on health care systems around the world. Expenditure on treating the condition is projected to rise to over £30 billion annually within the next three years. However, a recent study has shown that if the condition is diagnosed within four years of onset, it can be reversed by following a low-calorie diet. Limiting food intake to 600 calories per day for eight weeks was shown to have a lasting effect on the majority of subjects who took part in the trial. For many, Type 2 diabetes can be cured – and it need not cost the earth.

1 More than twice as many adults have Type 2 diabetes as did thirty years ago.

2 Nearly a third of people in the Pacific Islands have diabetes.

3 Type 2 diabetes is a long-term illness which can be caused by insufficient insulin production.

4 The increase in Type 2 diabetes is partly due to greater life expectancy.

## QUESTIONS 5–7

*Complete the sentences 5–7 using NO MORE THAN THREE WORDS from the passage above.*

5 Treating diabetes places a significant _____ on health care budgets.

6 If a person _____ with diabetes early, he or she can be cured.

7 Most people _____ in the low-calorie diet study made a good recovery.

# 3 Education

## Vocabulary

### Academic subjects:

- **archaeology** also **archeology**
  UNCOUNTABLE NOUN **Archaeology** is the study of the societies and peoples of the past by examining the remains of their buildings, tools, and other objects. ▪ *an archaeology professor at Florida State University*

- **astronomy**
  UNCOUNTABLE NOUN **Astronomy** is the scientific study of the stars, planets, and other natural objects in space. ▪ *a 10-day astronomy mission*

- **economics**
  UNCOUNTABLE NOUN **Economics** is the study of the way in which money, industry, and trade are organized in a society.
  ▪ *He gained a first class Honours degree in economics.* ▪ *having previously studied economics and fine art*

- **geology**
  UNCOUNTABLE NOUN **Geology** is the study of the Earth's structure, surface, and origins. ▪ *He was visiting professor of geology at the University of Jordan.*

- **linguistics**
  UNCOUNTABLE NOUN **Linguistics** is the study of the way in which language works.
  ▪ *Modern linguistics emerged as a distinct field in the nineteenth century.*

- **psychology**
  UNCOUNTABLE NOUN **Psychology** is the scientific study of the human mind and the reasons for people's behaviour. ▪ *Professor of Psychology at Bedford College* ▪ *research in educational psychology*

- **sociology**
  UNCOUNTABLE NOUN **Sociology** is the study of society or of the way society is organized. ▪ *a sociology professor at the University of North Carolina* ▪ *a treatise on the sociology of religion*

### Academic activities:

- **analyse (analyses, analysing, analysed)**
  VERB If you **analyse** something, you consider it carefully or use statistical methods in order to fully understand it. [US **analyze**]
  ▪ *McCarthy was asked to analyse the data from the first phase of trials of the vaccine.*
  ▪ *[+ what] This book teaches you how to analyse what is causing the stress in your life.*

- **claim (claims, claiming, claimed)**
  VERB If you say that someone **claims that** something is true, you mean they say that it is true but you are not sure whether or not they are telling the truth. ▪ *[+ that] He claimed that it was all a conspiracy against him.* ▪ *[+ to-inf] A man claiming to be a journalist threatened to reveal details about her private life.* ▪ *He claims a 70 to 80 per cent success rate.*

- **define (defines, defining, defined)**
  VERB If you **define** a word or expression, you explain its meaning, for example in a dictionary. ▪ *[+ as] Collins English Dictionary defines a workaholic as 'a person obsessively addicted to work'.*

- **evaluate (evaluates, evaluating, evaluated)**
  VERB If you **evaluate** something or someone, you consider them in order to make a judgment about them, for example about how good or bad they are. ▪ *They will*

first send in trained nurses to evaluate the needs of the individual situation. ▪ *The market situation is difficult to evaluate.* ▪ [+ *how*] *we evaluate how well we do something*

- **investigate (investigates, investigating, investigated)**
  VERB If you investigate something, you study or examine it carefully to find out the truth about it. ▪ *Research in Oxford is now investigating a possible link between endometriosis and the immune system.* ▪ [+ *how*] *Police are still investigating how the accident happened.*

## Nouns associated with research:

- **evidence**
  UNCOUNTABLE NOUN **Evidence** is anything that you see, experience, read, or are told that causes you to believe that something is true

or has really happened. ▪ [+ *of/for*] *a report on the scientific evidence for global warming* ▪ [+ *that*] *There is a lot of evidence that stress is partly responsible for disease.* ▪ [+ *to-inf*] *To date there is no evidence to support this theory.*

- **hypothesis (hypotheses)**
  NOUN A **hypothesis** is an idea which is suggested as a possible explanation for a particular situation or condition, but which has not yet been proved to be correct. [FORMAL] ▪ *Work will now begin to test the hypothesis in rats.* ▪ *Different hypotheses have been put forward to explain why these foods are more likely to cause problems.*

- **theory (theories)**
  NOUN A **theory** is a formal idea or set of ideas that is intended to explain something. ▪ [+ *of*] *Einstein formulated the Theory of Relativity in 1905.*

# Practice exercises

**Exam tip:** Words for academic subjects can have many different endings, but these are common.

| –ics: *statistics* | –logy: *biology* | –y: *philosophy* |
| --- | --- | --- |

Learn to recognize these.

1  Complete words 1–7 below with the ending –ics, –logy, or –y to form the names of subjects. Then match them to the topics of study a–g.

| | | | | |
| --- | --- | --- | --- | --- |
| **1** | archaeo _____ | | **a** | the human mind |
| **2** | astronom _____ | | **b** | people of the past |
| **3** | econom _____ | | **c** | society |
| **4** | geo _____ | | **d** | money, industry and trade |
| **5** | linguist _____ | | **e** | the Earth |
| **6** | psycho _____ | | **f** | how language works |
| **7** | socio _____ | | **g** | stars and planets |

**Exam tip:** Words for naming people by their occupations often end in *–er.*
      Examples: *teacher/farmer/miner*
Words for naming people who study academic subjects for a living usually end in *–ist.*
      Examples: *biologist/physicist*
Learn to recognize these.

2 Choose the correct words for academic subjects and the people who study them to complete sentences 1–7.

1 An _____ at the Royal Observatory has discovered a new moon in our solar system.

2 She wanted to understand why people feel, think, and behave in certain ways, so she decided to do a degree in _____.

3 _____ is the study of language in general, not any particular language such as French or Mandarin.

4 The government's predictions for economic growth and inflation were not endorsed by leading _____.

5 Students from the department of _____ spent the weekend studying rock formations off the coast of Scotland.

6 Graduates in _____ often take jobs which involve analysing data and formulating social policy.

7 _____ were called in to investigate the Iron Age tools discovered on the building site.

> **Exam tip:** When writing in the IELTS exam you need to use not only the right words but also the right parts of speech, for example:
>
> *Thompson and her colleagues analyse (verb) the samples using the antibody test.*
> *The main results of the analysis (noun) are summarized below.*
> *I have an analytical (adjective) approach to every survey.*
>
> When you learn a new word, learn its associated parts of speech.

3 The words in the table are commonly linked to academic study. Use your dictionary to complete the table.

| verb | noun | adjective |
|---|---|---|
| claim | | × |
| | definition | × |
| evaluate | | |
| | investigation | |
| × | evidence | |
| | hypothesis | |
| | | theoretical |

4 Choose the correct part of speech from the words in italics for sentences 1–6.

1 When giving a presentation, it is important to *define/definition* key terms.

2 An effective essay is not just descriptive but also *evaluation/evaluative*.

3 It is important to *investigate/investigation* the causes of inequality.

4 It is now *evidence/evident* that stress contributes to disease.

5 Most scientific research begins with a *hypothesize/hypothesis*.

6 There is no *theory/theoretical* model to explain the impact of inflation on economic growth.

**5** Choose words from the table in Exercise 3 to complete the sentences 1–5.

**1** In academic discussions, it is important to _____ arguments for their strengths and weaknesses.

**2** It would be difficult to design a scientific experiment to test the _____ that multiple time dimensions exist.

**3** To date there is no _____ to support this theory.

**4** After lengthy _____, they were still unable to identify the source of the leak.

**5** There is no general agreement on a standard _____ of the term 'intelligence'.

# Exam practice: Writing Task 2

Below is a student's answer to an IELTS Writing Task 2, in which candidates are required to write a 250 word essay on a given topic. Complete the essay with words from the unit. There may be more than one correct answer. Hint: make sure you choose the correct part of speech.

## WRITING TASK 2

**Write about the following topic:**

*Is there any value in studying academic subjects that are not 'useful' in terms of generating wealth for the country?*

**Give reasons for your answer and include any relevant examples from your own knowledge or experience.**

**Write at least 250 words.**

Many people these days (1) _____ that a useful education is one that prepares graduates for occupations that create wealth. However, when we (2) _____ the usefulness of an academic subject we should think carefully about how we (3) _____ the term 'useful'. In this essay, I argue that many academic subjects that do not directly generate great wealth can still be very useful.

Some subjects can be useful because they create knowledge that can be applied in related fields. (4) _____, for example, study the way language works. Their (5) _____ can be used to create more effective methods of language teaching. Improved international communication can result in better trading relations, which can in turn generate wealth. (6) _____ (7) _____ the lives of people in the past through their artifacts. Many of these will be displayed in museums, which can attract tourists who generate income for hoteliers, restaurants and so on.

Many academic subjects can also be 'useful' in terms of contributing to people's quality of life. Some people pursue hobbies in fields such as (8) _____ in order to have a better understanding of the planet we live on. Others with an interest in stars and planets may become amateur (9) _____. Curiosity is an important human trait, and many academic subjects allow people to satisfy this need.

In short, there is little (10) _____ that simply educating people to be efficient workers makes them happier or richer in the broader sense. Human curiosity and the unpredictable nature of knowledge creation mean that a variety of academic disciplines should be valued.

**Now complete the essay in your own words.**

# 4 Adventure

## Vocabulary

### Verbs associated with travel and adventure:

- **accompany (accompanies, accompanying, accompanied)**
  VERB If you **accompany** someone, you go somewhere with them. [FORMAL] ▪ *Ken agreed to accompany me on a trip to Africa.* ▪ *The Prime Minister, accompanied by the governor, led the President up to the house.*

- **encounter (encounters, encountering, encountered)**
  VERB If you **encounter** problems or difficulties, you experience them. ▪ *Every day of our lives we encounter stresses of one kind or another.* ▪ *Environmental problems they found in Poland were among the worst they encountered.*

- **overcome (overcomes, overcoming, overcame)**
  VERB If you **overcome** a problem or a feeling, you successfully deal with it and control it. ▪ *Molly had fought and overcome her fear of flying.* ▪ *One way of helping children to overcome shyness is to boost their self-confidence.*

- **reschedule (reschedules, rescheduling, rescheduled)**
  VERB If someone **reschedules** an event, they change the time at which it is supposed to happen. ▪ *Since I'll be away, I'd like to reschedule the meeting.* ▪ *[+ for] They've rescheduled the opening for February 14th.*

- **seek (seeks, seeking, sought)**
  VERB If you **seek** something, you try to find it or obtain it. [FORMAL] ▪ *Four people who sought refuge in the Italian embassy have left voluntarily.* ▪ *[+ for] Candidates are urgently sought for the post of Conservative Party chairman.* ▪ *Always seek professional legal advice before entering into any agreement.* ▪ *[+ from] The couple have sought help from marriage guidance counsellors.*

- **venture (ventures, venturing, ventured)**
  VERB If you **venture** somewhere, you go somewhere that might be dangerous. [LITERARY] ▪ *People are afraid to venture out for fear of sniper attacks.*

### Nouns associated with travel and adventure:

- **challenge (challenges)**
  NOUN A **challenge** is something new and difficult which requires great effort and determination. ▪ *I like a big challenge and they don't come much bigger than this.* ▪ *The new government's first challenge is the economy.*

- **destination (destinations)**
  NOUN The **destination** of someone or something is the place to which they are going or being sent. ▪ *Spain is still our most popular holiday destination.* ▪ *Only half of the emergency supplies have reached their destination.*

- **itinerary (itineraries)**
  NOUN An **itinerary** is a plan of a journey, including the route and the places that you will visit. ▪ *The next place on our itinerary was Silistra.*

- **journey (journeys)**
  NOUN When you make a **journey**, you travel from one place to another. ▪ *[ + to ] There is an express service from Paris which completes the journey to Bordeaux in under 4 hours.*

## Adjectives to describe experiences:

- **dreary**
  ADJECTIVE If you describe something as **dreary**, you mean that it is dull and depressing. ▪ *a dreary little town in the Midwest*

- **intense**
  ADJECTIVE **Intense** is used to describe something that is very great or extreme in strength or degree. ▪ *He was sweating from the intense heat.* ▪ *His threats become more intense, agitated, and frequent.*

- **pivotal**
  ADJECTIVE A **pivotal** role, point, or figure in something is one that is very important and affects the success of that thing. ▪ *The Court of Appeal has a pivotal role in the English legal system.* ▪ *The elections may prove to be pivotal in Colombia's political history.*

- **profound**
  ADJECTIVE You use **profound** to emphasize that something is very great or intense. ▪ *discoveries which had a profound effect on many areas of medicine* ▪ *The overwhelming feeling is just deep, profound shock and anger.* ▪ *Anna's patriotism was profound.*

- **valuable**
  ADJECTIVE If you describe something or someone as **valuable**, you mean that they are very useful and helpful. ▪ *Many of our teachers also have valuable academic links with Heidelberg University.* ▪ *The experience was very valuable.*

## Practice exercises

**1** Listen to speakers 1–6 describing their adventures. Indicate which of the verbs a–g each speaker uses by writing a letter in the spaces below:

04

| | | |
|---|---|---|
| **a** | accompany | Speaker 1 _____ |
| **b** | reschedule | Speaker 2 _____ |
| **c** | venture | Speaker 3 _____ |
| **d** | encounter | Speaker 4 _____ |
| **e** | overcome | Speaker 5 _____ |
| **f** | seek | Speaker 6 _____ |

**Exam tip:** You can improve your mark in the IELTS Speaking exam if you learn to pronounce words correctly.

For multi-syllable words it is important to get the stress pattern right.

When you learn a new word, learn which syllable is pronounced most strongly.

Listen again to speakers 1–6 in Exercise 1. Underline the stressed syllable of each key verb a–f. Practise saying the words out loud.

2  **Look at these pairs of words with similar meanings. Complete the sentence pairs 1–8 with words from the table.**

| | |
|---|---|
| itinerary | journey |
| encounter | meet |
| pivotal | significant |
| seek | look for |
| intense | profound |
| dreary | dull |
| valuable | priceless |
| destination | goal |

**1**  **a**  You can use the expression _____ if you are trying to find something.

   **b**  _____ is a more formal word that you can use if you are trying to find something that is quite important, a job for example.

**2**  **a**  If something is _____, it is boring and depressing.

   **b**  If something is _____, it is not interesting or exciting.

**3**  **a**  Your _____ is the place that you hope to reach.

   **b**  Your _____ is something that you hope to achieve.

**4**  **a**  If you _____ someone, you may come across them unexpectedly or because you have arranged to get together.

   **b**  If you _____ someone, you come across them, usually unexpectedly.

**5**  **a**  When you make a _____, you travel from one place to another.

   **b**  An _____ is the plan you make before you travel.

**6**  **a**  If something is _____, it is very meaningful and may affect the way you think and feel.

   **b**  If something is _____, it is extreme in strength or degree.

**7**  **a**  A _____ role, point or figure in something is one that is important.

   **b**  A _____ role, point or figure in something is one that is very important and affects the success of that thing.

**8**  **a**  If something is _____, it is very useful and/or worth a lot of money.

   **b**  If something is _____, it is extremely useful and/or worth a great deal of money.

**3**   Choose words from the table of pairs in Exercise 2 to complete the sentences 1–8.

   **1**   According to our _____ we should be in Zanzibar by 8.30 Tuesday evening.

   **2**   Many people travel to the tropics, _____–*ing* sun and adventure.

   **3**   Their _____ through Africa was one that they had been looking forward to for years.

   **4**   If you travel without making reservations, you are likely to _____ problems.

   **5**   Our trip to the coast was rather _____ as it was overcast and the beaches were dirty.

   **6**   Retrieving my stolen passport was a _____ moment – after that, everything went smoothly.

   **7**   After exploring the caves, we're going to _____ my cousin and his wife at the local bar.

   **8**   Seeing the poverty in that part of the word was a very _____ experience – it made me sad and thoughtful.

## Exam practice: Speaking Part 2

In Part 2 of the IELTS Speaking exam you have to speak for one to two minutes about a topic you are given. You will receive a task card like the one below. You have one minute to prepare what to say and to make a few written notes if you wish.

**For this practice exercise, listen to the model answer and write down seven target words from Unit 4 that the speaker uses.**

05

Describe an adventure that you have had, either at home or abroad.
You should say:
        what you did
        why you did it
        how you felt about it
and explain what you learned from the experience.

**When you are ready, try the exercise yourself. Before you speak, note down four to eight key words.**

**Tip:** Make sure you have studied the definitions and sample sentences for your key words carefully.

# 5  Gadgets

## Vocabulary

### Nouns to describe dimensions:

- **angle (angles)**
  NOUN An **angle** is the difference in direction between two lines or surfaces. Angles are measured in degrees. ▪ *The boat is now leaning at a 30 degree angle.*

- **circumference**
  UNCOUNTABLE NOUN The **circumference** of a circle, place, or round object is the distance around its edge. ▪ *a scientist calculating the Earth's circumference* ▪ *The island is 3.5 km in circumference.*

- **diameter (diameters)**
  NOUN The **diameter** of a round object is the length of a straight line that can be drawn across it, passing through the middle of it. ▪ *[+ of] a tube less than a fifth of the diameter of a human hair* ▪ *a length of 22-mm diameter steel pipe*

- **height (heights)**
  NOUN The **height** of a person or thing is their size or length from the bottom to the top. ▪ *Her weight is about normal for her height.* ▪ *I am 5'6'' in height.* ▪ *[+ of] The tree can grow to a height of 20ft.* ▪ *He was a man of medium height.*

- **length (lengths)**
  NOUN The **length** of something is the amount that it measures from one end to the other along the longest side. ▪ *It is about a metre in length.* ▪ *[+ of] the length of the field* ▪ *[+ of] The plane had a wing span of 34ft and a length of 22ft.*

- **radius (radii)**
  NOUN The **radius** around a particular point is the distance from it in any direction.

▪ *[+ around] Nigel has searched for work in a ten-mile radius around his home.* ▪ *[+ of] within a fifty-mile radius of the town* ▪ *Fragments of twisted metal were scattered across a wide radius.*

- **volume (volumes)**
  NOUN The **volume of** something is the amount of it that there is. ▪ *[+ of] Senior officials will be discussing how the volume of sales might be reduced.* ▪ *[+ of] the sheer volume of traffic and accidents*

- **width (widths)**
  NOUN The **width** of something is the distance it measures from one side or edge to the other. ▪ *[+ of] Measure the full width of the window.* ▪ *The road was reduced to 18ft in width by adding parking bays.* ▪ *Saddles are made in a wide range of different widths.*

### Actions:

- **adjust (adjusts, adjusting, adjusted)**
  VERB When you **adjust to** a new situation, you get used to it by changing your behaviour or your ideas. ▪ *[+ to] We are preparing our fighters to adjust themselves to civil society.* ▪ *[+ to] I felt I had adjusted to the idea of being a mother very well.*

- **convey (conveys, conveying, conveyed)**
  VERB To **convey** information or feelings means to cause them to be known or understood by someone. ▪ *Semiological analysis sees a sign as any cultural symbol which conveys a meaning.* ▪ *In every one of her pictures she conveys a sense of immediacy.* ▪ *He also conveyed his views and the views of the bureaucracy.*

- **launch (launches, launching, launched)**
  VERB If a company **launches** a new product, it makes it available to the public. ▪ *Crabtree & Evelyn has just launched a new jam, Worcesterberry Preserve.* ▪ *Marks & Spencer recently hired model Linda Evangelista to launch its new range.*

- **reinforce (reinforces, reinforcing, reinforced)**
  VERB If something **reinforces** a feeling, situation, or process, it makes it stronger or more intense. ▪ *A stronger European Parliament would, they fear, only reinforce the power of the larger countries.* ▪ *This sense of privilege tends to be reinforced by the outside world.*

- **secure (secures, securing, secured)**
  VERB If you **secure** something that you want or need, you obtain it, often after a lot of effort. [FORMAL] ▪ *Federal leaders continued their efforts to secure a ceasefire.* ▪ *Graham's achievements helped secure him the job.*

- **suspend (suspends, suspending, suspended)**
  VERB If you **suspend** something, you delay it or stop it from happening for a while or until a decision is made about it. ▪ *The union suspended strike action this week.* ▪ [+ *until*] *A U.N. official said aid programs will be suspended until there's adequate protection for relief convoys.*

## Practice exercises

1   Match the words a–h to pictures 1–8.

| **a** angle | **c** diameter | **e** length | **g** volume |
|---|---|---|---|
| **b** circumference | **d** height | **f** radius | **h** width |

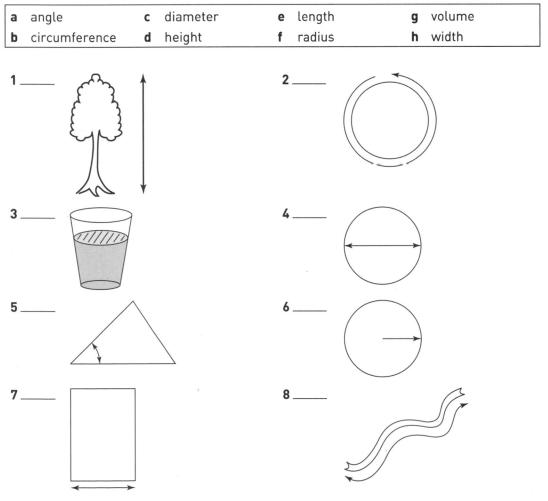

1 _____

2 _____

3 _____

4 _____

5 _____

6 _____

7 _____

8 _____

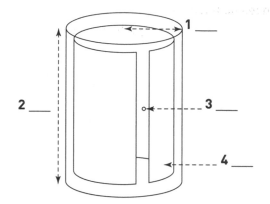

🎧 **2** Listen to the description of the pinhole camera and complete the diagram by writing the correct dimensions in gaps 1–4.

06

---

**Exam tip:** Many words in English have more than one meaning.

You need to pay attention to the context so that you interpret words correctly. Collocations (words that commonly go together) can help you recognize which meaning of a word is intended in that context.

Example: *If you **convey goods** from one place to another you carry or transport them. If you **convey a message** you make it understood.*

Learn to recognize collocations and the multiple meanings of words.

---

**3** Use the words from the box to complete sentence pairs 1–5.

| adjust | launch | reinforce | secure | suspend |
|---|---|---|---|---|

**1** **a** We had to _____ the meeting because the fire alarm went off unexpectedly.

   **b** If you _____ the light directly above the object, you will see it's shape more clearly.

**2** **a** When we noticed the bulge in the wall, we had to call in the builders to _____ it.

   **b** He produced some good data to _____ his argument.

**3** **a** You'll have to _____ that camera lens to get a clear image.

   **b** It took me several years to _____ to the climate in Nairobi.

**4** **a** Few countries have the facilities to _____ a rocket into space.

   **b** The company are hoping to _____ the new phone in time for Christmas.

**5** **a** In order to buy a house, you have to _____ a loan.

   **b** if you want the bookcase to stay in place, you should _____ it to the wall.

**4** Listen to sentences 1–5, which contain the verbs from exercise 3. Indicate the meaning of the verb in bold by circling a or b.

**1** In this sentence does **adjust** mean:

    **a** change something to make it more effective? Or

    **b** get used to something?

**2** In this sentence does **launch** mean:

    **a** send something into the air? Or

    **b** make something available to the public?

**3** In this sentence does **reinforce** mean:

    **a** make something stronger? Or

    **b** give evidence to support an idea?

**4** In this sentence does **secure** mean:

    **a** obtain? Or

    **b** fasten?

**5** In this sentence does **suspend** mean:

    **a** stop or delay an activity? Or

    **b** hang something?

## Exam practice: Listening – labelling a diagram – classifying

You are going to hear three students talking about a project for a course in product design. They have been instructed to create a device which will convey a ping-pong ball between two tables positioned a metre apart. Listen and match the suggestions with the person who makes them by writing the correct letter A, B or C next to questions 1–6.

**Exam tip:** Listen for collocations and context to recognize the meaning of key verbs.

    **A** Lisa                **B** Bill                **C** Omar

**1** project the ball into the air _____

**2** hang a paper bridge between the tables _____

**3** fasten the strips of paper together with clips _____

**4** tie the bridge to the table _____

**5** create a tube from the strips of paper _____

**6** make the structure stronger _____

# 6   Cities

## Vocabulary

### Nouns:

- **amenity (amenities)**
  NOUN Amenities are things such as shopping centres or sports facilities that are provided for people's convenience, enjoyment, or comfort. ▪ *The hotel amenities include health clubs, conference facilities, and banqueting rooms.*

- **commuter (commuters)**
  NOUN A **commuter** is a person who travels a long distance to work every day. ▪ *The number of commuters to London has dropped by 100,000.*

- **congestion**
  UNCOUNTABLE NOUN If there is **congestion** in a place, the place is extremely crowded and blocked with traffic or people. ▪ *The problems of traffic congestion will not disappear in a hurry.* ▪ *Energy consumption, congestion and pollution have increased.*

- **housing**
  UNCOUNTABLE NOUN You refer to the buildings in which people live as housing when you are talking about their standard, price, or availability. ▪ *a shortage of affordable housing*

- **resident (residents)**
  NOUN The **residents** of a house or area are the people who live there. ▪ *The Archbishop called upon the government to build more low cost homes for local residents.* ▪ *More than 10 percent of Munich residents live below the poverty line.*

- **immigrant (immigrants)**
  NOUN An **immigrant** is a person who has come to live in a country from some other country. ▪ *industries that employ large numbers of illegal immigrants* ▪ *Portugal, Spain and Italy all have large immigrant populations from Africa.*

- **infrastructure (infrastructures)**
  NOUN The **infrastructure** of a country, society, or organization consists of the basic facilities such as transport, communications, power supplies, and buildings, which enable it to function. ▪ *investment in infrastructure projects* ▪ *a focus on improving existing infrastructure*

- **inhabitant (inhabitants)**
  NOUN The **inhabitants** of a place are the people who live there. ▪ [+ of] *the inhabitants of Glasgow* ▪ *Jamaica's original inhabitants were the Arawak Indians.*

- **neighbourhood (neighbourhoods)**
  NOUN A **neighbourhood** is one of the parts of a town where people live. [US **neighborhood**] ▪ [+ to-inf] *It seemed like a good neighbourhood to raise my children.* ▪ [+ of] *He was born and grew up in the Flatbush neighbourhood of Brooklyn.*

### Adjectives:

- **bustling**
  ADJECTIVE A **bustling** place is full of people who are very busy or lively. ▪ *the bustling streets of Salzburg* ▪ *Oxford was bustling with students and tourists and shoppers.*

- **pioneering**
  ADJECTIVE **Pioneering** work or a **pioneering** individual does something that has not been done before, for example by developing or using new methods or

techniques. ▪ *The school has won awards for its pioneering work with the community.* ▪ *a pioneering Scottish surgeon and anatomist named John Hunter*

- **historic**
  ADJECTIVE Something that is **historic** is important in history or is likely to be important. ▪ *The opening of the Scottish Parliament was a historic moment.* ▪ *a fourth historic election victory*

- **rural**
  ADJECTIVE **Rural** means relating to country areas as opposed to large towns. ▪ *These*

plants have a tendency to grow in the more rural areas. ▪ *the closure of rural schools*

- **sprawling**
  ADJECTIVE A place that is **sprawling** has been built over a large area in an untidy or uncontrolled way ▪ *a sprawling suburb on the edge of a big city* ▪ *The house was a sprawling ranch-style building.*

- **urban**
  ADJECTIVE **Urban** means belonging to, or relating to, a town or city. ▪ *Most of the population is an urban population.* ▪ *Most urban areas are close to a park.* ▪ *urban planning*

## Practice exercises

> **Exam tip:** In the IELTS Reading exam you may have to answer questions about the writer's attitude.
>
> Writers often convey their attitude by choosing words which have positive, negative or neutral connotations, for example:
>
> If a writer describes a solution as *simple*, they mean that it is obvious and straightforward (positive connotation). If a writer describes a solution as *simplistic*, they are criticizing it for being simpler than it should be (negative connotation).
>
> Learn to recognize whether a word has a positive, negative or neutral connotation.

1   Sentences 1–5 contain pairs of words in italics which are similar in meaning. Underline the word in italics which has the more positive connotation.

1   The shopping centre is normally *crowded/bustling* on a Saturday afternoon.

2   The roads are *busy/congested* during rush hour.

3   That housing scheme has won awards for its *novel/pioneering* design.

4   The city centre is surrounded by *extensive/sprawling* suburbs.

5   There are many *old/historic* buildings in the town centre.

> **Exam tip:** In the IELTS Reading exam you may have to show that you can identify the writer's main ideas by matching headings to sections of text.
>
> The headings capture the main ideas, and the sections contain detailed information and examples. Superordinates (words that describe a group or category) can help you match headings.
>
> For example, in the word set: *summer, season, winter, and spring*, the word *season* is the superordinate term because *summer, winter and spring* are examples ▪ of seasons.
>
> Learn to recognize superordinate terms.

**2** For each set of words or expressions 1–4, circle the superordinate term.

| | | | |
|---|---|---|---|
| **1** underground train | public transport | tram | commuter rail |
| **2** housing | flat | bungalow | council house |
| **3** library | leisure centre | park | amenity |
| **4** power supply | roads | infrastructure | communications |

**3** Choose the correct superordinate term 1–3 for words a–h below. Write the correct number 1–3 next to words a–h.

**1** people
**2** places
**3** events

**a** commuter
**b** immigrant
**c** suburb
**d** region
**e** street party
**f** resident
**g** inhabitant
**h** neighbourhood

**4** Read the paragraph below. Which of the superordinate terms 1–4 matches the words in bold?

**1** *Quantity* of food consumed in New York

**3** *Origin* of food consumed in New York

**2** *Quality* of food consumed in New York

**4** *Types* of food consumed in New York

As in many urban areas, seventy per cent of the food consumed in New York is imported from **overseas**. Most of the remainder is produced in rural areas elsewhere in the **country**. Only a tiny percentage of food is produced in the **city** itself – mainly soft fruit and vegetables grown in patches of **ground** between buildings or on rooftop **gardens**. If New Yorkers used their green spaces more efficiently, they could produce up to twenty per cent of the fruit and vegetables they eat.

## Exam practice: Reading – matching headings

*The reading passage opposite has 5 paragraphs, A–E.*

*Choose the correct heading for paragraphs B–E from the list of headings below. Write the correct numbers i-viii in spaces 1–4 at the top of the page.*

*NB There are more headings than paragraphs, so you will not use them all.*

### List of headings

**i** The quality of urban housing

**ii** Amenities in urban areas

**iii** The affordability of urban housing

**iv** The amenities that people want

**v** The urban-rural divide

**vi** The quality of rural infrastructure

**vii** Rural neighbourhoods in the city

**viii** Rural transport

*Example:* Paragraph A    *Answer: v*

  **1**  Paragraph B  _____
  **2**  Paragraph C  _____
  **3**  Paragraph D  _____
  **4**  Paragraph E  _____

## The lure of the urban village

**A**

Many people dream of leaving the city and moving to the countryside, but in fact we are an overwhelmingly urban population. Over 80 per cent of UK residents now live in urban areas. Globally, it's much the same; according to the United Nations, by 2012, well over half of the world's population will be living in towns and cities.

**B**

Increasingly, people are living in towns, but what many really want is a piece of the countryside within the town. Three years ago a survey of 1,000 homeowners in the UK found that many of those who were planning to relocate wanted to live near gyms, shops and restaurants. Today, according to a more recent report, the majority want a crime-free neighbourhood, a back garden, and theatre or gallery within reach. The report concludes that Britons are becoming more concerned about their quality of life and are willing to prioritize tranquillity over status and salary.

**C**

However, what the report does not say is that, for people without a high salary the chances of buying the ideal house, or indeed any house at all in the city, are becoming increasingly slim. According to recent figures, even if we take inflation into account, average urban house values are four times higher than they were 70 years ago. A comparison of average house prices and average incomes is even less favourable. Since 1940, home price rises have far exceeded rises in average salaries.

**D**

For those who can, moving to the countryside is an option. In most developed countries, the roads, power supply and communication facilities are adequate for their needs. Indeed, improvements in telecommunications make telecommuting an increasingly attractive proposition.

**E**

Those forced to stay behind in urban life are increasingly yearning for neighbourhoods that are 'village' like in feel. Indeed those who market new homes are increasingly using such terms to attract buyers. Interestingly, the idea of urban villages is not a new one. The term was coined 50 years ago, by the American sociologist Herbert Gans in his study of the Italian-American communities of Boston. According to Gans, the communities he studied refashioned urban space in an attempt to recreate the intimate feel of the Southern Italian villages they came from. He argued that American cities as a whole could be seen as a patchwork of different villages in which non-urban immigrants attempted to shape the city to resemble the places in the old country that they had left behind. His findings may well resonate with today's native urbanites yearning for village life.

# 7  The art of persuasion

## Vocabulary

### Reporting verbs:

- **advocate (advocates, advocating, advocated)**
VERB If you **advocate** a particular action or plan, you recommend it publicly. [FORMAL]
▪ *a conservative who advocates fewer government controls on business* ▪ *the tax policy advocated by the Opposition*

- **acknowledge (acknowledges, acknowledging, acknowledged)**
VERB If you **acknowledge** a fact or a situation, you accept or admit that it is true or that it exists. [FORMAL] ▪ [+ *that*]
*It is widely acknowledged that transferring knowledge in a classroom environment is very inefficient.* ▪ *Belatedly, the government has acknowledged the problem.*

- **assert (asserts, asserting, asserted)**
VERB If someone **asserts** a fact or belief, they state it firmly. [FORMAL] ▪ *The senator plans to assert that the bill violates the First Amendment.* ▪ *The defendants continue to assert their innocence.*

- **dispute (disputes, disputing, disputed)**
VERB If you **dispute** a fact, statement, or theory, you say that it is incorrect or untrue.
▪ *He disputed the allegations.* ▪ [+ *that*] *No one disputes that vitamin C is of great value in the treatment of scurvy.*

- **imply (implies, implying, implied)**
VERB If you **imply** that something is the case, you say something which indicates that it is the case in an indirect way. ▪ *'Are you implying that I had something to do with those attacks?'* ▪ *She was upset by the implied criticism.*

- **justify (justifies, justifying, justified)**
VERB To **justify** a decision, action, or idea means to show or prove that it is reasonable or necessary. ▪ *No argument can justify a war.* ▪ *Ministers agreed that this decision was fully justified by economic conditions.*

- **object (objects, objecting, objected)**
VERB If you **object** to something, you express your dislike or disapproval of it.
▪ [+ *to*] *A lot of people will object to the book.*
▪ [+ *that*] *Cullen objected that his small staff would be unable to handle the added work.*
▪ *We objected strongly but were outvoted.*

- **outline (outlines, outlining, outlined)**
VERB If you **outline** an idea or a plan, you explain it in a general way. ▪ *The mayor outlined his plan to clean up the town's image.*

- **question (questions, questioning, questioned)**
VERB If you **question** something, you have or express doubts about whether it is true, reasonable, or worthwhile. ▪ *Scientists began questioning the validity of the research because they could not reproduce the experiments.* ▪ *It never occurs to them to question the doctor's decisions.*

### Nouns associated with persuasion:

- **benefit (benefits)**
NOUN The **benefit of** something is the help that you get from it or the advantage that results from it. ▪ [+ *of*] *the benefits of this form of therapy* ▪ *For maximum benefit, use your treatment every day.* ▪ [+ *to*] *I hope what I have written will be of benefit to someone else.*

- **debate (debates)**
NOUN A **debate** is a discussion about a subject on which people have different views. ▪ *An intense debate is going on within*

the Israeli government. ▪ [+ about] There has been a lot of debate among scholars about this.

- **discussion (discussions)**
  NOUN If there is **discussion** about something, people talk about it, often in order to reach a decision. ▪ [+ about] There was a lot of discussion about the wording of the report. ▪ Council members are due to have informal discussions later on today.

- **drawback (drawbacks)**
  NOUN A **drawback** is an aspect of something or someone that makes them less acceptable than they would otherwise be. ▪ He felt the apartment's only drawback was that it was too small.

- **evidence**
  UNCOUNTABLE NOUN **Evidence** is anything that you see, experience, read, or are told that causes you to believe that something is true or has really happened. ▪ [+ of/for] the scientific evidence for global warming ▪ [+ that] There is a lot of evidence that stress is partly responsible for disease. ▪ [+ to-inf] To date there is no evidence to support this theory.

- **proof (proofs)**
  NOUN **Proof** is a fact, argument, or piece of evidence which shows that something is definitely true or definitely exists.
  ▪ [+ of] You have to have proof of residence in the state of Texas, such as a Texas ID card.
  ▪ Economists have been concerned with establishing proofs for their arguments.

## Practice exercises

> **Exam tip:** In the IELTS Writing exam you can demonstrate that you have a broad vocabulary by avoiding unnecessary repetition.
>
> Many words commonly used in academic arguments have synonyms.
>
> Example: *The minister* <u>justified</u> *his position on arms control. He* <u>defended</u> *his position strongly when he gave evidence of the proliferation of nuclear weapons.*
>
> Learn to use synonyms when presenting your arguments.

1 Match each word 1–4 with its closest synonym a–d.

| | | | |
|---|---|---|---|
| **1** | benefit | **a** | disadvantage |
| **2** | debate | **b** | discussion |
| **3** | drawback | **c** | evidence |
| **4** | proof | **d** | advantage |

2 Find words in the text below which mean:

1 recommend publicly (verb)
2 accept the existence or truth of (verb)
3 proven to be reasonable or necessary (adjective)
4 explain in a general way (verb)
5 disapprove of (verb)

There has been considerable debate among politicians over whether the use of force to protect human rights can ever be justified. Some advocate the use of arms as the only way of sending a clear message to oppressive regimes. Others object to the use of force on humanitarian grounds, arguing that it inevitably results in the loss of innocent lives. While it is important to acknowledge that there are compelling arguments on both sides, I would suggest that a range of responses should be considered when there is proof that human rights are under threat. In this essay I will outline three such responses.

> **Exam tip:** In the IELTS Writing exam you should make sure that you use words correctly.
>
> Some of the words in this unit can be followed by:
>
> a preposition, for example: *One of the benefits of the new phone is a larger screen.*
>
> *whether* + clause, for example: *I doubt whether the new policy on care for the elderly can succeed.*
>
> *that* + clause, for example: *We suggested that the working day should be reduced.*
>
> a noun or noun phrase, for example: *They cannot justify their actions.*
>
> Learn to use words correctly by studying example sentences.

3 **Match the beginning of each sentence 1–5 with the most appropriate ending a–e.**

| | | | |
|---|---|---|---|
| **1** | There has been some debate | **a** | to the new motorway. |
| **2** | The advertisers acknowledged | **b** | over whether tuition fees should be increased. |
| **3** | Campaigners have objected | **c** | of the current system is that it rewards excessive risk-taking. |
| **4** | One of the drawbacks | **d** | whether the government's new policy on alcohol will work. |
| **5** | Opposition politicians question | **e** | that they had misrepresented their product. |

4 **Report the statements 1–5 using the verbs a–e.**

| | | | |
|---|---|---|---|
| **a** acknowledge | **c** object | **e** imply |
| **b** dispute | **d** question | **f** assert |

1 'We have some doubts about the new printer. Will it really be more reliable than previous models?'

Consumers _____

2 'We are completely against the sale of national treasures abroad.'

Many people _____

3 'Yes, it is true that the National Health Service has improved the nation's health.'

Most people _____

4 'We strongly believe that new approaches to tackling youth crime should be explored.'

Some politicians _____

5 'These figures are not correct.'

Experts _____

6 'In the past, students who have achieved a mark of 70% or higher in the midterm test have always passed the course. Susan has achieved a mark of 75%, so...'

The teacher _____

# Exam practice: Writing – presenting an argument

For the IELTS Writing Task 2 you are required to write a 250-word essay on a given topic using your own knowledge and experience.

First study the text from Practice Exercise 2 as an example of how you might start your essay. Then read the dialogue below about freedom of speech. Use the words and expressions that you have learned in this unit in your response to the essay question below.

**Dialogue**

**Peter:** Of course there have to be limits to free speech! Even in the most democratic countries it is illegal to incite hatred – I mean to encourage people to harm others, minority groups for example.

**Felicity:** I disagree. Free speech is essential. The ability to tolerate different points of view is the hallmark of a civilized society.

**Karen:** I think you're both right to an extent. There may have to be some limits, but only in extreme circumstance. Basically, I think you have to let people speak freely because if you don't they may take to the streets and express their views in some possibly more destructive way – by rioting for example. Look at what happened in Eastern Europe in the 1980s – and in the Middle East today.

**Peter:** Well, yes, I suppose you have a point there...

**Karen:** Also, if you look at history, there are plenty of examples of people who have been silenced for ideas that are now accepted as true.

**Felicity:** That's right! Take Galileo, for example, who said that the earth revolves around the sun. He was punished by the authorities for his views.

WRITING TASK 2

**You should spend about 40 minutes on this task.**

**Write about the following topic:**

> *Is freedom of speech necessary in a free society?*

**Give reasons for your answer and include any relevant examples from your own knowledge or experience.**

**Write at least 250 words.**

A model answer is provided in the Answer key on page 105.

# 8   Getting involved

## Vocabulary

### Nouns:

- **current affairs**
PLURAL NOUN If you refer to **current affairs**, you are referring to political events and problems in society which are discussed in newspapers, and on television and radio.
▪ *people who take no interest in politics and current affairs* ▪ *the BBC's current affairs programme 'Panorama'*

- **recital (recitals)**
NOUN A **recital** is a performance of music or poetry, usually given by one person. ▪ *a solo recital by the famous harpsichordist*

- **drama (dramas)**
NOUN A **drama** is a serious play for the theatre, television, or radio. ▪ *He acted in radio dramas.*

### Adjectives:

- **amateur**
ADJECTIVE **Amateur** sports or activities are done by people as a hobby and not as a job.
▪ *the local amateur dramatics society*

- **classical**
ADJECTIVE You use **classical** to describe something that is traditional in form, style, or content. ▪ *Fokine did not change the steps of classical ballet; instead he found new ways of using them.* ▪ *the scientific attitude of Smith and earlier classical economists*

- **contemporary**
ADJECTIVE **Contemporary** things are modern and relate to the present time. ▪ *one of the finest collections of contemporary art in the country* ▪ *Only the names are ancient; the characters are modern and contemporary.*

### Verbs associated with involvement:

- **assemble (assembles, assembling, assembled)**
VERB When people **assemble** or when someone **assembles** them, they come together in a group, usually for a particular purpose such as a meeting. ▪ *There wasn't even a convenient place for students to assemble between classes.* ▪ [+ *in*] *Thousands of people assembled in a stadium in Thokoza.* ▪ *He has assembled a team of experts.*

- **attend (attends, attending, attended)**
VERB If you **attend** a meeting or other event, you are present at it. ▪ *Thousands of people attended the funeral.* ▪ *The meeting will be attended by finance ministers from many countries.*

- **broadcast (broadcasts, broadcasting)**
VERB To **broadcast** a programme means to send it out by radio waves, so that it can be heard on the radio or seen on television. ▪ [+ *on*] *The concert will be broadcast live on television and radio.*

- **establish (establishes, establishing, established)**
VERB If someone **establishes** something such as an organization, a type of activity, or a set of rules, they create it or introduce it in such a way that it is likely to last for a long time. ▪ *The U.N. has established detailed criteria for who should be allowed to vote.* ▪ *The school was established in 1989 by an Italian professor.*

- **observe (observes, observing, observed)**
VERB If you **observe** a person or thing,

you watch them carefully, especially in order to learn something about them.
▪ *Stern also studies and observes the behaviour of babies.* ▪ [+ how] *I got a chance to observe how a detective actually works.*

• **organize (organizes, organizing, organized)**
VERB If you **organize** an event or activity, you make sure that the necessary arrangements are made. [in Brit, also use **organise**] ▪ *The Commission will organize a conference on rural development.* ▪ *a two-day meeting organized by the United Nations* ▪ *The initial mobilization was well organized.*

• **participate (participates, participating, participated)**
VERB If you **participate** in an activity, you take part in it. ▪ [+ in] *Hundreds of faithful Buddhists participated in the annual ceremony.* ▪ [+ in] *Over half the population of this country participate in sport.* ▪ [V-ing] *lower rates for participating corporations*

• **resign (resigns, resigning, resigned)**
VERB If you **resign** from a job or position, you formally announce that you are leaving it. ▪ *A hospital administrator has resigned over claims he lied to get the job.* ▪ *Mr Robb resigned his position last month.*

## Practice exercises

**1** Listen to the radio programmes. Match the programmes with speakers 1–5 and write a–e in the spaces below.

09

Speaker 1 _____     **a** Current affairs programme

Speaker 2 _____     **b** sporting event

Speaker 3 _____     **c** classical music concert

Speaker 4 _____     **d** poetry recital

Speaker 5 _____     **e** radio drama

**2** Listen to another five speakers (1–5) describing their interests. Indicate each speaker's interest a–e and form of involvement i–iii in the table below.

10

**interest**                      **involvement**

**a** student magazine            **i** observer/spectator

**b** contemporary art            **ii** participant

**c** debating society            **iii** organizer

**d** classical music

**e** radio broadcasting

| | interest | involvement |
|---|---|---|
| Speaker 1 | | |
| Speaker 2 | | |
| Speaker 3 | | |
| Speaker 4 | | |
| Speaker 5 | | |

3   Match the more formal verbs a–e with their less formal equivalents i–v.

| | | | |
|---|---|---|---|
| **a** | attend | **i** | take part in |
| **b** | observe | **ii** | set up |
| **c** | participate | **iii** | put together |
| **d** | assemble | **iv** | go to |
| **e** | establish | **v** | watch |

4   Listen again to Track 10 on the CD. Indicate which of the verbs above each speaker uses by writing a letter a–e or a number i–v in the spaces below.

10

Speaker 1 _____

Speaker 2 _____

Speaker 3 _____

Speaker 4 _____

Speaker 5 _____

**5** Listen to the words 1–9 below. Indicate whether the 's' sounds like /s/ or /z/. Practise saying them.

| 1 | affairs | 4 | classical | 7 | orchestra |
|---|---------|---|-----------|---|-----------|
| 2 | assemble | 5 | establish | 8 | advise |
| 3 | broadcast | 6 | observe | 9 | resign |

**6** Write down five of your own interests. Check their pronunciation. Practise saying them out loud.

_____

_____

_____

_____

_____

## Exam practice: Speaking Part 1

In Part 1 of the IELTS Speaking exam you have to answer questions about everyday topics and common experiences.

For this practice exercise, listen to the recorded questions and sample answers.

When you are ready, listen to the questions again and give your own answers, using 2–3 sentences for each one. Pause the recording between each question to allow yourself time to answer.

# 9 Global warming

## Vocabulary

### Natural processes:

- **condense (condenses, condensing, condensed)**
  VERB When a gas or vapour **condenses**, or **is condensed**, it changes into a liquid.
  ▪ [+ to-inf] *Water vapour condenses to form clouds.* ▪ [+ into] *The compressed gas is cooled and condenses into a liquid.* ▪ [+ out of] *As the air rises it becomes colder and moisture condenses out of it.*

- **contract (contracts, contracting, contracted)**
  VERB When something **contracts** or when something **contracts** it, it becomes smaller or shorter. ▪ *Blood is only expelled from the heart when it contracts.* ▪ *New research shows that an excess of meat and salt can contract muscles.*

- **expand (expands, expanding, expanded)**
  VERB If something **expands** or **is expanded**, it becomes larger. ▪ *Engineers noticed that the pipes were not expanding as expected.* ▪ *The money supply expanded by 14.6 per cent in the year to September.* ▪ [V-ing] *a rapidly expanding universe*

- **flow (flows, flowing, flowed)**
  VERB If a liquid, gas, or electrical current **flows** somewhere, it moves there steadily and continuously. ▪ [+ into] *A stream flowed into the valley.* ▪ [+ into] *The current flows into electric motors that drive the wheels.*

### Verbs associated with scientific study:

- **estimate (estimates, estimating, estimated)** (also **overestimate, underestimate**)
  VERB If you **estimate** a quantity or value, you make an approximate judgment or calculation of it. ▪ [+ that] *The Academy of Sciences currently estimates that there are approximately one million plant varieties in the world.* ▪ *He estimated the speed of the winds from the degree of damage.*

- **predict (predicts, predicting, predicted)**
  VERB If you **predict** an event, you say that it will happen. ▪ *Chinese seismologists have predicted earthquakes this year in Western China.* ▪ [+ that] *Some analysts were predicting that online sales during the holiday season could top $10 billion.* ▪ [+ when] *tests that accurately predict when you are most fertile*

- **state (states, stating, stated)**
  VERB If you **state** something, you say or write it in a formal or definite way. ▪ *The table clearly states the amount of fat found in commonly used foods.* ▪ [+ that] *The police report stated that he was arrested for allegedly assaulting his wife.* ▪ *Buyers who do not apply within the stated period can lose their deposits.*

### Adjectives:

- **accurate** (opposite **inaccurate**)
  ADJECTIVE **Accurate** information, measurements, and statistics are correct to a very detailed level. An **accurate** instrument is able to give you information of this kind. ▪ *Accurate diagnosis is needed to guide appropriate treatment strategies.* ▪ *a quick and accurate way of monitoring the amount of carbon dioxide in the air*

- **likely** (opposite **unlikely**)
  ADJECTIVE You use **likely** to indicate that something is probably the case or will probably happen in a particular situation.

▪ *Experts say a 'yes' vote is still the likely outcome.* ▪ [+ that] *If this is your first baby, it's far more likely that you'll get to the hospital too early.*

## Nouns associated with climate:

- **current (currents)**
  1 NOUN A **current** is a steady and continuous flowing movement of some of the water in a river, lake, or sea. ▪ [+ of] *The ocean currents of the tropical Pacific travel from east to west.* ▪ *The couple were swept away by the strong current.*
  2 NOUN A **current** is a steady flowing movement of air. ▪ [+ of] *a current of cool air* ▪ *The spores are very light and can be wafted by the slightest air current.*

- **drought (droughts)**
  NOUN A **drought** is a long period of time during which no rain falls. ▪ *Drought and famines have killed up to two million people here.*

- **flood (floods)**
  NOUN If there is a **flood**, a large amount of water covers an area which is usually dry, for example when a river flows over its banks or a pipe bursts. ▪ *More than 70 people were killed in the floods, caused when a dam burst.* ▪ *Floods hit Bihar state, killing 250 people.*

- **glacier (glaciers)**
  NOUN A **glacier** is an extremely large mass of ice which moves very slowly, often down a mountain valley. ▪ *University of Alaska scientists report that the state's glaciers are melting faster than expected.* ▪ *Twenty thousand years ago, the last great ice age buried the northern half of Europe under a massive glacier.*

- **hurricane (hurricanes)**
  NOUN A **hurricane** is an extremely violent wind or storm. ▪ *In September 1813, a major hurricane destroyed US gunboats and ships that were defending St Mary's, Georgia, from the British.* ▪ *Around eight hurricanes are predicted to strike America this year.*

- **typhoon (typhoons)**
  NOUN A **typhoon** is a very violent tropical storm. ▪ *large atmospheric disturbances such as typhoons* ▪ *a powerful typhoon that killed at least 32 people*

## Practice exercises

1 Complete each sentence 1–6 with an appropriate word.

1 This mountain range was formed by _ l _ _ _ _ _s millions of years ago.

2 Tropical storms and _ y _ _ _ _ _ s are common in the South Pacific at this time of year.

3 The Horn of Africa has been afflicted with severe _ _ _ _ g _ _ s for many years.

4 You need to be careful when swimming in these waters as there's a very strong _ _ r _ _ _ t.

5 The cost of repairing properties damaged by the _ l _ _ _ ran into billions of pounds.

6 We've been advised to board up the windows and stay indoors as the _ u r _ _ _ _ _ _ is approaching fast.

🎧 2 Read the questions 1–4 about the words in Exercise 1. Then listen to Track 14 to find answers.
14

1 Is a hurricane more likely to cause a flood or a drought?

2 What is the difference between a hurricane and a typhoon?

3 Where might you find a glacier?

4 Where might you feel a current: in the air, in the water, in both air and water?

**3**   Make words 1–5 negative by adding a prefix.

  **1**   agree          **4**   legal

  **2**   consistent     **5**   responsible

  **3**   likely

**4**   Match the prefixes 1–4 with the word roots a–d.

  **1**   con-          **a**   –pand

  **2**   ex-           **b**   –estimate, -flow

  **3**   pre-          **c**   –dense, -tract

  **4**   over-         **d**   –historic

**5**   Choose words from exercises 3 and 4 to complete sentences 1–7. Make any necessary changes to verb forms.

  **1**   Water vapour _____ to form clouds.

  **2**   When water turns into ice, it _____ .

  **3**   In _____ times, people endured ice ages, that is prolonged periods of intense cold.

  **4**   During the flooding, rivers and streams _____ their banks in countless places.

  **5**   Climate scientists came to different conclusions because the data was _____ .

  **6**   Global warming is _____ to slow down in the near future.

  **7**   Politicians _____ over how to deal with climate change.

**6** Listen to sentence pairs 1–4. Complete the table with the antonyms that you hear.

| | sentence a | sentence b |
|---|---|---|
| 1 | | |
| 2 | | |
| 3 | | |
| 4 | | |

## Exam practice: Listening – completing notes

### QUESTIONS 1–9

Complete the notes below.

Write **NO MORE THAN THREE WORDS AND/OR A NUMBER** for each answer.
Hint: listen for antonyms and words with negative prefixes.

**Global warming today**
In earlier studies:

- some **1** _____ have been **overstated** but some **2** _____ have been **understated**

Risk factors:

- **3** _____ are **expected to** rise by 1m, not 2m
- Some **4** _____ and ice sheets seem **to be contracting**, e.g. Arctic; others seem **5** _____, e.g. Antarctic
- Gulf Stream is **6** _____ to vanish

Consequences:

- Tropical forests more vulnerable to **7** _____
- Hurricanes and **8** _____ are more severe
- Thawing permafrost is producing more methane

Conclusion:

- It is **irresponsible** to do nothing about **9** _____

# 10 Revision 1

## Practice exercises

1 Rewrite each sentence 1–5 using a word in box A for the expressions in bold and a word in box B for the expression in italics. You may have to make other changes to the sentence.

| A | clients, colleagues, employers, siblings, spouses |
|---|---|
| B | conventional, flexible, idealistic, tolerant, vulnerable |

1 My **brothers and sisters** *avoid doing anything out of the ordinary*.

2 **The people that I work with** *believe that different points of view should be respected*.

3 People **who are married to violent partners** are often *weak and unprotected*.

4 **The people that I work for** *adapt easily to new circumstances*.

5 **The people who use our services** *have very strong ideals*.

2 Listen to a doctor talking to five patients. Indicate each patient's health problem by writing a letter a–e in the spaces below:

| **a** allergy | **b** dehydration | **c** infection | **d** obesity | **e** stroke |
|---|---|---|---|---|

Patient 1 _____     Patient 4 _____

Patient 2 _____     Patient 5 _____

Patient 3 _____

3 Match the textbook extract 1–4 with the academic discipline a–f. There are two extra letters.

| **a** archaeology **b** astronomy **c** economics **d** geology **e** linguistics **f** sociology |
|---|

1 ... Many features can be explained with reference to plate tectonics. Mid-ocean ridges, elevated regions on the seafloor where volcanoes are situated, can be seen as divergent boundaries where two plates move apart... _____

2 ...Some argue that human agency, that is an individual's capacity to make free choices, determines human behaviour. Others maintain that human behaviour is largely determined by structural factors such as gender, ethnic origin, and social class, which limit the choices available to individuals... _____

3 ...Careful measurements have allowed us to develop a thorough understanding of minute gravitational changes and given us the ability to accurately determine past and future positions of the planets. More recently the tracking of objects near the Earth will make it possible to predict close encounters, and potential collisions, with the Earth... _____

4 ...According to the law of demand, in a given market there is generally an inverse relationship between price and quantity demanded. That is, all other factors being equal, the higher the price of a product, the less of it consumers are prepared to buy... _____

**4** **For each sentence 1–5 choose which sentence, a or b, is the closest paraphrase.**

1 We had to make some last-minute changes to our itinerary.

   **a** We had to exchange our money at the last minute.

   **b** We had to alter our travel plans at the last minute.

2 Learning to ride a motorcycle was a real challenge.

   **a** Learning to ride a motorcycle was great fun.

   **b** Learning to ride a motorcycle was quite difficult.

3 We had some strange encounters while touring the southern states.

   **a** We came across some unusual people while touring the southern states.

   **b** We travelled across some unusual countryside while touring the southern states.

4 Travelling to the Seychelles was a very valuable experience.

   **a** My journey to the Seychelles was very expensive.

   **b** My journey to the Seychelles was really worthwhile.

5 Quitting my job to travel round the world was a pivotal decision.

   **a** My life really changed when I decided to quit my job and travel round the world.

   **b** It was a private decision to quit my job and travel round the world.

**5** **Choose the object a, b or c that best fits the descriptions 1–6.**

1 This object is a container about seven centimetres in height. It has a diameter of ten centimetres across the top.

   **a** a wine bottle  **b** a tea cup  **c** a kettle

2 This is a very small but useful object, approximately 4 cm in length and 1 mm in width.

   **a** a nail file  **b** a memory stick  **c** a sewing needle

3 This object is usually made from a single length of wire, approximately 110 cm long, which has been formed into a flat oblong coil.

   **a** a drawing pin  **b** paper clip  **c** a coin

4 This object is about 1 m in length and can be adjusted to fit most adults of average size.

   **a** a belt  **b** a glove  **c** an umbrella

5 This object is normally about five or six centimetres in length and can be used to secure a room.

   **a** an electrical socket  **b** a light fixture  **c** a key

6 This is an object of variable length that may be used to suspend something from a height or to secure something such as a parcel.

   **a** a piece of string  **b** a length of wood  **c** a pair of scissors

**6** Choose the adjective a–e that best describes the place described by each speaker 1–5.

| a bustling | b historic | c rural | d sprawling | e urban |
|---|---|---|---|---|

Speaker 1 _____    Speaker 4 _____

Speaker 2 _____    Speaker 5 _____

Speaker 3 _____

**7** Listen to the extracts 1–5, and indicate whether the statements below are True or False.

**1** Speaker 1 justifies her decision to change her degree course. _____

**2** Speaker 2 acknowledges that his study partner has been a great help. _____

**3** Speaker 3 objects to the proposed increase in tuition fees. _____

**4** Speaker 4 implies that degree courses are much easier than they were in the past. _____

**5** Speaker 5 discusses the drawbacks of part-time study. _____

Then record yourself speaking for one minute in response to each question a–e:

**a** What is the most difficult decision you have ever had to make?

**b** Whose help and support would you most like to acknowledge and why?

**c** Tell me about something that's happening in the world to which you strongly object.

**d** To what extent has education in your country changed over the last 20 years?

**e** What are some of the benefits and drawbacks of your place of work or study?

**8** Read the passage below and underline words and expressions which are similar in meaning to expressions 1–6.

| 1 were present at | 3 arranged | 5 take part in |
|---|---|---|
| 2 modern | 4 television and radio | 6 non-professional |

There is a popular belief that during hard economic times, people turn to entertainment for diversion and escape. If this were true, the entertainment industry should be booming. Figures released today suggest that it isn't.

Fewer people attended the cinema last year than in any of the preceding ten years. Theatre, dance, and live music, both classical and contemporary, saw similar declines, with not only lower attendance but also fewer events organized. Curiously enough, broadcast media have also failed to gain materially from the economic downturn. Audience figures for both radio and television programmes have remained broadly similar over the last three years.

There is, however, a silver lining to this cloud. Whilst fewer people appear to be attending cultural events, there has been a small but significant rise in the number of people choosing to participate in such activities. Amateur dramatics, poetry recitals, and debating societies have all enjoyed something of a comeback after many years of steady decline...

9

16

Listen again to Track 16, the lecture on global warming in the Exam practice section of Unit 9. Use the lecture notes below to write a response to this Writing Task 2 question.

*Should the international community do more to tackle the threat of global warming?*

**Global warming today**

In earlier studies:

- Some risk factors overstated, but some consequences understated

Risk factors:

- Sea levels expected to rise by 1m, not 2m
- Some glaciers and ice sheets contracting, e.g. Arctic; others expanding, e.g. Antarctic
- Gulfstream unlikely to vanish

Consequences:

- Tropical forests more vulnerable to drought
- Hurricanes and typhoons more severe

Conclusion:

- Irresponsible to do nothing about global warming

A model answer is provided in the Answer key on page 106

# 11 Words for describing graphs and figures

## Vocabulary

### Nouns for graphs and figures:

- **bar chart (bar charts)**
  NOUN A **bar chart** is a graph which uses parallel rectangular shapes to represent changes in the size, value, or rate of something or to compare the amount of something relating to a number of different countries or groups. [mainly UK; US **bar graph**] ▪ *The bar chart below shows the huge growth of U.K. car exports over the past few years.*

- **diagram (diagrams)**
  NOUN A **diagram** is a simple drawing which consists mainly of lines and is used, for example, to explain how a machine works. ▪ *Each tube enters the muscle wall of the uterus (see diagram on page 20).*

- **flow chart (flow charts)**
  NOUN A **flow chart** or a **flow diagram** is a diagram which represents the sequence of actions in a particular process or activity. ▪ [+ *of*] *a flow chart of the process* ▪ *Design a flow chart to explain the registration process.*

- **line graph (line graphs)**
  NOUN A **line graph** is a diagram that shows the relationship between two sets of changing numbers or measurements. ▪ *Begin by drawing the axes of a standard line graph.* ▪ *The line graph shows the degree and direction of change over time.*

- **pie chart (pie charts)**
  NOUN A **pie chart** is a circle divided into sections to show the relative proportions of a set of things. ▪ *The pie chart above shows how much more Britain has saved in shares than bonds.* ▪ *The pie chart indicates that one company has emerged as the dominant market share leader.*

- **table (tables)**
  NOUN A **table** is a written set of facts and figures arranged in columns and rows. ▪ *Consult the table on page 104.* ▪ *Other research supports the figures in Table 3.3.*

### Components of graphs and figures:

- **axis (horizontal/vertical) (axes)**
  NOUN An **axis** of a graph is one of the two lines on which the scales of measurement are marked. When you describe a graph, you refer to the line along the bottom of the graph as the **horizontal axis** and the line down the side of the graph as the **vertical axis**. ▪ *The vertical axis shows the level of the students' knowledge and the horizontal axis shows the length of the course in weeks.*

- **column (columns)**
  NOUN On a printed page such as a page of a dictionary, newspaper, or printed chart, a **column** is one of two or more vertical sections which are read downwards. ▪ [+ *of*] *We had stupidly been looking at the wrong column of figures.*

- **key (keys)**
  NOUN The **key** on a graph, chart, or diagram is a list of the symbols, abbreviations, or colours used and their meanings. For example, the **key** for a chart might show that the figures for girls are red and the figures for boys are blue.

- **row (rows)**
  NOUN A **row of** things or people is a number of them arranged in a line. ▪ [+ *of*] *a row of plants* ▪ *Several men are pushing school desks and chairs into neat rows.*

- **segment (segments)**
  NOUN A **segment** of a circle is one of the two parts into which it is divided when you draw a straight line through it. ▪ *Divide the circle into segments like an orange.* ▪ *The pie chart is divided into equal segments.*

- **step (steps)**
  NOUN A **step** is one of a series of actions that you take in order to achieve something. ▪ [+ *towards*] *He greeted the agreement as the first step towards peace.* ▪ *The next step is to put the theory into practice.*

### Verbs meaning 'show':

- **depict (depicts, depicting, depicted)**
  If a graph or diagram **depicts** something, it is shown there in the form of lines, shapes, or figures. ▪ *Reading from left to right, the first four columns depict our transactions with customers.*

- **represent (represents, representing, represented)**
  VERB If a sign or symbol **represents** something, it is accepted as meaning that thing. ▪ *A black dot in the middle of the circle is supposed to represent the source of the radiation.*

## Practice exercises

**1** Match expressions a–g with pictures 1–7.

| | | | | | | | |
|---|---|---|---|---|---|---|---|
| **a** | bar chart | **c** | flow chart | **e** | map | **g** | table |
| **b** | diagram | **d** | line graph | **f** | pie chart | | |

**1**

**2**

**4**

**5**
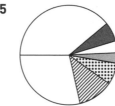

**7**
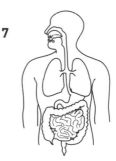

**3**

**6**

**2** Indicate the type of graph or figure a–g in Exercise 1 that you would use to represent the kinds of information 1–7 below. Write a letter a–g in each space.

**1** Steps in the process of recruiting staff for a company: _____

**2** The number of children vaccinated for measles over a 30-year period: _____

**3** The percentage breakdown of a country's total working population by ethnic origin: _____

**4** The layout of a university campus: _____

**5** A solar-powered hot water system: _____

**6** Percentage of male and female police officers in six cities across the UK: _____

**7** Sales figures for ten different types of mobile phone in twelve retail outlets: _____

**3** Words 1–9 can be used to describe parts of graphs or figures. Complete the table by writing numbers 1–9 in the boxes. Some words may be used more than once.

| 1 | arrow | 4 | horizontal axis | 7 | segment |
|---|-------|---|-----------------|---|---------|
| 2 | bar | 5 | key | 8 | step |
| 3 | column | 6 | row | 9 | vertical axis |

| bar chart | diagram | flow chart | line graph | map | pie chart | table |
|-----------|---------|------------|------------|-----|-----------|-------|
| | | | | | | |

> **Exam tip:** For the IELTS Writing Task 1 you have to summarize information that is usually represented in the form of a table, a pie chart, a line graph, a bar chart, a diagram, a map or a flow chart. You should write at least 150 words and organize your work carefully into three separate parts:
>
> • An **opening paragraph** briefly describing what the graph or figure shows (1–3 sentences)
>
> • **Body paragraph(s)** highlighting the key information
>
> • A **concluding paragraph** summarizing the most important point (1–2 sentences)

**4** Passages 1–7 are examples of introductory paragraphs of Writing Task 1 essays. Complete the passages with words and expressions from exercises 1, 2 and 3.

**1** The _____ shows the online university application procedure. The process consists of six _____.

**2** The _____ depicts the city of Milan. As can be seen from the _____, the dark shaded areas represent industrial zones, and the light shaded areas represent commercial zones.

**3** The _____ compares the literacy levels of primary school pupils at age eleven in thirteen schools across the country. Attainment is indicated along the _____ axis, and the schools are listed on the horizontal axis.

**4** The _____ illustrates how a telescope works. The _____ on the right show the direction of light as it passes through the lens.

**5** The _____ shows the percentage breakdown of company employees by salary. There are five _____, each of which represents a salary range from £10,000 to £35,000.

**6** The _____ represents the number of international students enrolled at Australian universities over a 30-year period. The vertical axis represents numbers of students in units of a thousand. The _____ axis lists the years between 1980 and 2010.

**7** The _____ gives data for accident and emergency hospital admissions. There are five _____ representing the five most common reasons for hospital admission and seven rows giving figures for seven different city hospitals.

> **Exam tip:** Certain standard words frequently appear in Writing Task 1 essays, for example:
>
> The graph _shows_... The number of ... _decreased_.
>
> Show that you have a broad vocabulary by using synonyms where possible, for example:
>
> _The number of hours worked _decreased_ slightly between 1985 and 1990, levelled off, then _dipped_ again briefly in 1997._

**5** Look again at passages 1–7 in exercise 4. Underline five words or expressions which are used as synonyms for the word 'shows'.

## Exam practice: Writing Task 1

### Writing Task 1

**You should spend about 20 minutes on this task.**

_The charts below show local government expenditure in 2000 and 2010._

_Summarize the information by selecting and reporting the main features, and make comparisons where relevant._

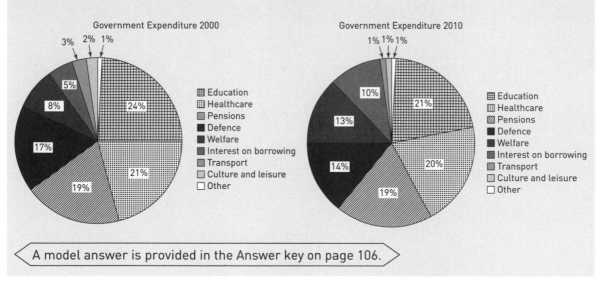

A model answer is provided in the Answer key on page 106.

# 12 Words for describing change

## Vocabulary

### Verbs associated with change:

- **abandon (abandons, abandoning, abandoned)**
  VERB If you **abandon** an activity or piece of work, you stop doing it before it is finished.
  ▪ *The authorities have abandoned any attempt to distribute food.* ▪ *The scheme's investors, fearful of bankruptcy, decided to abandon the project.*

- **adjust (adjusts, adjusting, adjusted)**
  VERB When you **adjust to** a new situation, you get used to it by changing your behaviour or your ideas. ▪ *[+ to] We are preparing our fighters to adjust themselves to civil society.* ▪ *[+ to] I felt I had adjusted to the idea of being a mother very well.*

- **alter (alters, altering, altered)**
  VERB If something **alters** or if you **alter** it, it changes. ▪ *Little had altered in the village.*
  ▪ *attempts to genetically alter the caffeine content of coffee plants*

- **decline (declines, declining, declined)**
  VERB If something **declines**, it becomes less in quantity, importance, or strength.
  ▪ *[+ from] The number of staff has declined from 217,000 to 114,000.* ▪ *Hourly output by workers declined 1.3% in the first quarter.*
  ▪ *[V-ing] a declining birth rate*

- **develop (develops, developing, developed)**
  VERB When something **develops**, it grows or changes over a period of time and usually becomes more advanced, complete, or severe. ▪ *It's hard to say at this stage how the market will develop.* ▪ *[+ into] These clashes could develop into open warfare.*

- **diminish (diminishes, diminishing, diminished)**
  VERB When something **diminishes**, or when something **diminishes** it, it becomes reduced in size, importance, or intensity.
  ▪ *The threat of nuclear war has diminished.*
  ▪ *Federalism is intended to diminish the power of the central state.* ▪ *[V-ing] Universities are facing grave problems because of diminishing resources.* ▪ *This could mean diminished public support for the war.*

- **evolve (evolves, evolving, evolved)**
  VERB If something **evolves** or you **evolve** it, it gradually develops over a period of time into something different and usually more advanced. ▪ *[+ into] a tiny airline which eventually evolved into Pakistan International Airlines* ▪ *[+ from] Popular music evolved from folk songs.* ▪ *As medical knowledge evolves, beliefs change.*

- **modify (modifies, modifying, modified)**
  VERB If you **modify** something, you change it slightly, usually in order to improve it.
  ▪ *The club members did agree to modify their recruitment policy.* ▪ *The plane was a modified version of the C-130.*

- **refine (refines, refining, refined)**
  VERB If something such as a process, theory, or machine **is refined**, it is improved by having small changes made to it.

■ *Surgical techniques are constantly being refined.* ■ *Twentieth century botanists have continually refined these classifications.*

- **shift (shifts, shifting, shifted)**
  VERB If someone's opinion, a situation, or a policy **shifts** or **is shifted**, it changes slightly. ■ *Attitudes to mental illness have shifted in recent years.* ■ *The emphasis should be shifted more towards Parliament.*

- **transform (transforms, transforming, transformed)**
  VERB To **transform** something or someone means to change them completely and suddenly so that they are much better or more attractive. ■ *The spread of the internet and mobile telephony have transformed society.* ■ *[+ into] Yeltsin was committed to completely transforming Russia into a market economy.*

## Nouns for periods of time:

- **century (centuries)**
  1 NOUN A **century** is any period of a hundred years. ■ *The drought there is the worst in a century.* ■ *[+ of] This may be ending centuries of tradition.*
  2 NOUN A **century** is a period of a hundred years that is used when stating a date. For example, the 19th century was the period from 1801 to 1900. ■ *celebrated figures of the late eighteenth century* ■ *a 17th-century merchant's house*

- **decade (decades)**
  NOUN A **decade** is a period of ten years, especially one that begins with a year ending in 0, for example 1980 to 1989. ■ *the last decade of the nineteenth century*

- **generation (generations)**
  NOUN A **generation** is all the people in a group or country who are of a similar age, especially when they are considered as having the same experiences or attitudes. [ *+ of* ] *the younger generation of Party members* ■ *David Mamet has long been considered the leading American playwright of his generation.*

- **millennium (millenniums or millennia)**
  NOUN A **millennium** is a period of one thousand years, especially one which begins and ends with a year ending in '000', for example the period from the year 1000 to the year 2000. [FORMAL] ■ *But then many Japanese companies are unsure whether they will survive until the new millennium at all.* ■ *France begins celebrating the millennium an hour before Britain, and Eurotunnel wants to make sure supplies are maintained.*

## Practice exercises

**1** Listen to exam candidates 1–6 answering questions about changes. In the left-hand column, write which verb a–f is used by each candidate 1–6.

20

Candidate 1 _____        **a** abandon _____
Candidate 2 _____        **b** adjust _____
Candidate 3 _____        **c** decline _____
Candidate 4 _____        **d** develop _____
Candidate 5 _____        **e** evolve _____
Candidate 6 _____        **f** modify _____

> **Exam tip:** Similar words can have a positive, negative or neutral meaning, depending on the context they are used in.
>
> Example: the words *intricate, complicated* and *complex* can all be used to describe something that has many parts. However:
>
> *Intricate* usually has a more positive connotation and is often used to describe decorative objects:
>
>> *The fireplace was carved with intricate patterns.*
>
> *Complicated* usually has a more negative connotation and is often used to describe situations that are difficult to understand or deal with:
>
>> *The situation in Lebanon is very complicated.*
>
> *Complex* is generally more neutral in tone and is often used to describe things that are challenging to understand:
>
>> *These complex machines can perform a variety of tasks.*
>
> Learning to use words with positive, negative, and neutral connotations can help you express your ideas and attitudes more effectively.

🎧 **2** Listen again to candidates 1–6 in Exercise 1 on Track 20. Indicate whether the verbs a–f in
**20** Exercise 1 have a positive, negative or neutral connotation in that context by writing: +, – or 0 next to each verb.

**3** The words below all refer to periods of time. Rewrite them in order beginning with the shortest time period and ending with the longest.

| century | decade | generation | millennium | year |
|---|---|---|---|---|

🎧 **4** Verbs 1–5 below can also refer to changes. Indicate whether they usually have a positive,
**21** negative or neutral connotation by writing +, – or 0 in the spaces. Then listen to speakers 1–5 to check your answers. Listen again and write the time expression each speaker uses which includes the words from exercise 3.

| word | connotation | time expression |
|---|---|---|
| **1** alter | | *five centuries ago* |
| **2** diminish | | |
| **3** refine | | |
| **4** shift | | |
| **5** transform | | |

**5** Use words from exercises 1–4 to talk about changes in your own country. Use words with a positive connotation to talk about positive changes. Use words with a negative connotation to talk about negative changes. Use neutral verbs for changes that you feel are neither positive nor negative.

**Exam tip:** Improve your pronunciation by focusing on problem consonants.

Depending on your language, these may include:

- consonants which come at the end of a word, for example: *develop*
- groups of consonants with no vowels between them (consonant clusters), for example: *evolve*
- closely-related consonant sounds which are not differentiated in your language, for example: /b/ and /v/; /l/ and /r/; /s/ and /θ/

Practise saying words which end with consonant sounds.

Practise saying words with consonant clusters until you can say them without adding extra vowels.

If you have difficulty differentiating between two sounds, practise repeating word pairs which only differ in those sounds, for example, for /l/ and /r/, practise saying *light* and *right*.

**6** Listen to Track 22 and repeat words 1–15. Identify words with problem consonants and practise saying them until you can pronounce them clearly.

22

## Exam practice: Speaking Part 3

**Exam tip:** In Part 3 of the IELTS Speaking exam you have to discuss the topic of Part 2 with the examiner.

The examiner will ask you questions that will allow you to analyse issues and express opinions.

Some of these questions may require you to compare past and present and to speculate about future changes.

Learning to talk confidently about change can help you perform well in Part 3 of the Speaking exam.

For this practice exercise, you will hear three questions related to the topic of Unit 4: Adventure. Record yourself answering the questions.

23

Listen to your responses and answer questions 1–2 below:

1 Have you conveyed your attitude effectively by correctly using words with positive, negative and neutral connotations?

2 Have you pronounced consonant sounds clearly?

Listen to the sample answers and try the exercise again.

24

# 13 Words expressing similarity and difference

## Vocabulary

### Verbs for describing difference:

- **contrast (contrasts, contrasting, contrasted)**
VERB If you **contrast** one thing **with** another, you point out or consider the differences between those things. ▪ [+ with] *She contrasted the situation then with the present crisis.* ▪ *In this section we contrast four possible broad approaches.*

- **differ (differs, differing, differed)**
VERB If two or more things **differ**, they are unlike each other in some way.
▪ [+ from] *The story he told police differed from the one he told his mother.*
▪ *Management styles differ.*

- **differentiate (differentiates, differentiating, differentiated)**
VERB If you **differentiate between** things or if you **differentiate** one thing **from** another, you recognize or show the difference between them. ▪ [+ between] *A child may not differentiate between his imagination and the real world.* ▪ [+ from] *At this age your baby cannot differentiate one person from another.*

- **distinguish (distinguishes, distinguishing, distinguished)**
VERB If you can **distinguish** one thing **from** another or **distinguish between** two things, you can see or understand how they are different. ▪ [+ from] *Asteroids are distinguished from meteorites in terms of their visibility.* ▪ [+ between] *Research suggests that babies learn to see by distinguishing between areas of light and dark.*

- **vary (varies, varying, varied)**
VERB If things **vary**, they are different from each other in size, amount, or degree.
▪ *Assessment practices vary in different schools or colleges.* ▪ [+ from] *The text varies from the earlier versions.* ▪ [V-ing] *Different writers will prepare to varying degrees.*

### Verbs for describing similarity:

- **compare (compares, comparing, compared)**
VERB When you **compare** things, you consider them and discover the differences or similarities between them. ▪ *Compare the two illustrations in Fig 60.* ▪ [+ with] *Was it fair to compare independent schools with state schools?* ▪ [+ to] *Note how smooth the skin of the upper arm is, then compare it to the skin on the elbow.*

- **resemble (resembles, resembling, resembled)**
VERB If one thing or person **resembles** another, they are similar to each other.
▪ *Some of the commercially produced venison resembles beef in flavour.* ▪ *It is true that both therapies do closely resemble each other.*

### Adjectives and adverbs for describing difference:

- **contrary**
ADJECTIVE Ideas, attitudes, or reactions that are **contrary to** each other are completely different from each other.
▪ [+ to] *This view is contrary to the aims of critical social research for a number of*

reasons. • *Several of those present had contrary information.* • *people with contrary interests*

- **conversely**
ADVERB You say **conversely** to indicate that the situation you are about to describe is the opposite or reverse of the one you have just described. [FORMAL] • *If government saving is high private saving will be low. Conversely if government saving is negative then private saving will be high.* • *That makes Chinese products even cheaper and, conversely, makes American-made goods more expensive to export.*

- **distinct**
ADJECTIVE If something is **distinct from** something else of the same type, it is different or separate from it. •[+ *from*] *Engineering and technology are disciplines distinct from one another and from science.* • *This book is divided into two distinct parts.*

- **diverse**
ADJECTIVE If a group or range of things is **diverse**, it is made up of a wide variety of things. • *a diverse range of habitats* • *Society is now much more diverse than ever before.*

## Adjectives for describing similarity:

- **alike**
ADJECTIVE If two or more things are **alike**, they are similar. • *The two brothers look very alike.*

- **comparable**
ADJECTIVE Something that is **comparable** to something else is roughly similar, for example in amount or importance. • *paying the same wages to men and women for work of comparable value* • [+ *to*] *Farmers were meant to get an income comparable to that of townspeople.*

- **equivalent**
ADJECTIVE Something that is **equivalent** has the same value as another thing. • [+ *to*] *A unit is equivalent to a glass of wine or a single measure of spirits.* • *They will react with hostility to the price rises and calls for equivalent wage increases are bound to be heard.*

- **identical**
ADJECTIVE Things that are **identical** are exactly the same. • [+ *to*] *The new buildings look identical to those built 200 years ago.* • *The two parties fought the last election on almost identical manifestos.*

## Practice exercises

**1**  Circle the words for describing similarity.  Underline the words for describing difference.

| | | | |
|---|---|---|---|
| **a** | alike | **e** | distinct |
| **b** | comparable | **f** | diverse |
| **c** | contrary | **g** | equivalent |
| **d** | conversely | **h** | identical |

**2**  Listen and complete sentences 1–8 using words a–h above.

25

**1**  Victor and Vincent are _____ twins.

**2**  Boys and girls rarely think _____.

**3**  We enjoy watching a _____ range of films.

**4**  Psychiatry and psychology are two _____ disciplines.

**5**  The average cost of a house today is _____ to six years' average annual salary.

**6**  The minister was sacked for expressing views that were _____ to those of the government.

**7** The majority of female respondents reported spending more on sugary snacks; _____, the majority of male respondents said they had spent more on savoury snacks.

**8** People who do similar work should receive _____ rates of pay.

**3** Each group of words below contains a pair of synonyms. Circle the odd word out.

**1** differentiate       differ       distinguish

**2** identical       similar       analogous

**4** Choose words from Exercise 3 to complete the sentences below.

You can (1) _____ or (2) _____ *between* two things; however, we normally say that one thing (3) _____ *from* something else.

If two things are exactly the same we can say that they are (4) _____; if they are somewhat the same we can say they are (5) _____ or (6) _____.

> **Exam tip:** When questions in the IELTS Listening exam require you to write one or more words you need to make sure that you use the correct part of speech.
>
> When you learn a new word, learn its associated parts of speech.

**5** Use your dictionary to complete the table below. There may be more than one answer in some cases.

| verb | noun | adjective | adverb |
| --- | --- | --- | --- |
| compare | | | |
| contrast | | | |
| differ | | | |
| resemble | | × | × |
| vary | | | |

**6** Listen to sentences 1–7. Circle the words in the table above that you hear.

**7** Listen to Track 26 again. Complete the summary of each sentence 1–7 below using one of the words you have circled. Make any necessary changes to verb forms.

**1** Eating a _____ diet is vital.

**2** The dangers involved in flying and sailing are _____.

**3** His choice was based on my _____ of the programmes.

**4** The _____ between the two songs was notable.

**5** The students understood the task _____.

**6** His online views are often in _____ to his televised views.

**7** Three economic crises were _____.

# Exam practice: Listening – completing a summary

**Exam tip:** When completing a summary in the IELTS Listening exam you should write words that you hear in the gaps.

However, the words that you see around the gaps in the summary are likely to be synonyms of the words that you hear.

Example:　　　You see: *Teachers often find it <u>difficult</u> to _____ students' abilities.*
　　　　　　　You hear: *Educators often find it <u>challenging</u> to assess students' abilities.*

When preparing to listen, underline key words in the summary and anticipate synonyms.

## QUESTIONS 1–5

Complete the summary below. Write **NO MORE THAN THREE WORDS AND/OR A NUMBER** for each answer.

### JOB STRESS VS JOB CHALLENGE

Many people experience job stress and describe the workplace as challenging. However, 'stress' and 'challenge' are not (1) _____ terms. Job stress results when the requirements of a job outstrip the workers capacities. Challenging work is (2) _____ from stressful work because a challenge encourages the individual to develop capabilities in a healthy way. Meeting a challenge is (3) _____ to the idea of stretching in order to reach for a goal. Two workers could have very (4) _____ experiences of identical jobs because no two people are (5) _____.

# 14 Words describing cause and effect

## Vocabulary

### Nouns:

- **chain reaction (chain reactions)**
  NOUN A **chain reaction** is a series of events, each of which causes the next. ▪ *Whenever recession strikes, a chain reaction is set into motion.* ▪ *[+ of] The powder immediately ignited and set off a chain reaction of explosions.*

- **consequence (consequences)**
  NOUN The **consequences of** something are the results or effects of it. ▪ *[+ of] Her lawyer said she understood the consequences of her actions and was prepared to go to jail.* ▪ *[+ for] An economic crisis may have tremendous consequences for our global security.*

- **impact (impacts)**
  NOUN The **impact** that something has **on** a situation, process, or person is a sudden and powerful effect that it has on them. ▪ *[+ on] the mining industry's devastating impact on the environment* ▪ *an area where technology can make a real impact*

- **influence (influences)**
  NOUN To have an **influence on** people or situations means to affect what they do or what happens. ▪ *[+ on] Van Gogh had a major influence on the development of modern painting.* ▪ *Many other medications have an influence on cholesterol levels.*

- **outcome (outcomes)**
  NOUN The **outcome** of an activity, process, or situation is the situation that exists at the end of it. ▪ *Mr. Singh said he was pleased with the outcome.* ▪ *[+ of] It's too early to know the outcome of her illness.* ▪ *a successful outcome*

- **repercussion (repercussions)**
  NOUN If an action or event has **repercussions**, it causes unpleasant things to happen some time after the original action or event. [FORMAL] ▪ *It was an effort which was to have painful repercussions.* ▪ *Members of congress were warned of possible repercussions if their vote went through.*

### Verbs:

- **affect (affects, affecting, affected)**
  VERB If something **affects** a person or thing, it influences them or causes them to change in some way. ▪ *Nicotine from cigarettes can adversely affect the heart.* ▪ *More than seven million people have been affected by drought.* ▪ *The new law will directly affect thousands of people.*

- **contribute (contributes, contributing, contributed)**
  VERB If something **contributes to** an event or situation, it is one of the causes of it. ▪ *[+ to] The report says design faults in both the vessels contributed to the tragedy.* ▪ *[V-ing] Stress, both human and mechanical, may also be a contributing factor.*

- **determine (determines, determining, determined)**
  VERB If a particular factor **determines** the nature of a thing or event, it causes it to be of a particular kind. [FORMAL] ▪ *IQ is strongly determined by genetic factors.* ▪ *[+ whether] What determines whether you are a career success or a failure?*

- **generate (generates, generating, generated)**
  VERB To **generate** something means to cause it to begin and develop. ▪ *The Employment Minister said the reforms would generate new jobs.* ▪ *the excitement generated by the changes in Eastern Europe*

- **induce (induces, inducing, induced)**
  VERB To **induce** a state or condition means to cause it. ▪ *Doctors said surgery could induce a heart attack.* ▪ *an economic crisis induced by high oil prices*

- **provoke (provokes, provoking, provoked)**
  VERB If something **provokes** a reaction, it causes it. ▪ *His election success has provoked a shocked reaction.* ▪ *The destruction of the mosque has provoked anger throughout the Muslim world.*

- **result (results, resulting, resulted)**
  VERB If something **results in** a particular situation or event, it causes that situation or event to happen. ▪ [+ *in*] *Fifty per cent of road accidents result in head injuries.* ▪ [+ *in*] *Continuous rain resulted in the land becoming submerged.*

- **stem (stems, stemming, stemmed)**
  VERB If a condition or problem **stems from** something, it was caused originally by that thing. ▪ [+ *from*] *Much of the instability stems from the economic effects of the war.* ▪ [+ *from*] *Much of London's energy and resilience stems from the fact that London has always been a city that relied on migrants.*

- **trigger (triggers, triggering, triggered)**
  VERB If something **triggers** an event or situation, it causes it to begin to happen or exist. ▪ *the incident which triggered the outbreak of the First World War* ▪ *The current recession was triggered by a slump in consumer spending.*

## Practice exercises

1   Sentences 1–9 contain words or expressions in bold which indicate a cause and effect relationship. For each sentence, underline the cause and put brackets around the effect.

  **1**   One of the **consequences** of the growth of social networking is a reduction of government control of information.

  **2**   Critics fear that tax rises will have a number of undesirable **repercussions** including a slowdown in investment.

  **3**   Better maternal health is just one of the **outcomes** of the government's reform of services.

  **4**   The collapse of the bank set off a **chain reaction** of financial crises throughout the country.

  **5**   The company's insolvency **stems from** a series of poor decisions made five years ago.

  **6**   His statements about corruption in the police **provoked** an immediate response.

> **Exam tip:** You do not need to know all of the vocabulary in the IELTS Reading exam.
>
> You can often work out the meaning of a word by looking at the context. If you do not understand a word or expression, you can look for:
>
> **a**   a superordinate term; for example if you don't understand *endives*: *Britons these days eat* <u>*endives*</u>*, rocket, and sprouting broccoli,* **vegetables** *that a generation ago were unheard of.*
>
> **b**   examples; for example if you don't understand *artefacts*: <u>*Artefacts*</u> *such as* **tools, jewellery and containers,** *can help us understand ancient civilizations whose history is not recorded in writing.*
>
> **c**   a synonym or definition; for example if you don't understand *drowsiness*: *This drug can induce* <u>*drowsiness*</u>*, that is* **difficulty staying awake.**
>
> **d**   an antonym; for example if you don't understand *anxious*: *Some children can be* **relaxed** *at home but* <u>*anxious*</u> *at school.*

**2** For each sentence 1–4 use the context to write the meaning of the words in bold. Underline the words that help explain the words in bold and indicate whether they are:

    **a** a superordinate term       **c** a synonym or definition

    **b** an example            **d** an antonym

**1** We saw that whereas the original photo showed the complete scene, the published version had been **cropped**.

**2** Air quality can be improved through greater use of **catalytic converters**, devices which reduce pollution generated by cars.

**3** Rocket launchers, **grenades** and other weapons were discovered under the floorboards.

**4** Some researchers have employed a **flawed** methodology, for example failing to adequately consider significant variables.

**3** Words and expressions 1–9 all appear in bold in the reading passage. Study the context in which they appear and circle the meaning a or b in the table which best defines the word as it is used in the passage.

## Birth Order and Personality

The belief that birth order has a lasting **impact** on personality is widespread and frequently referred to in popular psychology literature. Alfred Adler (1870 – 1937), an Austrian psychotherapist, was one of the first to argue that birth order **contributes to** the formation of character. He **maintained** that firstborn children could often be profoundly affected by the loss of status brought about by the birth of siblings. Eldest children, according to Adler, **were prone to** be both anxious and conscientious, that is, inclined to work hard, perhaps in order to regain a position of **primacy** within the family.

Since Adler, there have been numerous attempts to verify the **influence** of birth order on a range of personality **traits**, in particular: rebelliousness, conscientiousness, extroversion, agreeableness, and anxiety. Some studies have found that last born children tend to be more extrovert and **agreeable**, that is, they not only seek out the company of others but also tend to get along well with other people. Middle children, on the other hand, are least likely to **be compliant**. They tend to rebel, perhaps in an attempt to define themselves as 'special' in relation to their more conscientious elder siblings and agreeable younger siblings.

| **1** impact | **a** cause | **b** effect |
|---|---|---|
| **2** contributes to | **a** is one of the causes | **b** is one of the effects |
| **3** maintained | **a** denied | **b** believed |
| **4** were prone to | **a** had a tendency to | **b** were unlikely to |
| **5** primacy | **a** greatest importance | **b** least importance |
| **6** influence | **a** effect | **b** cause |
| **7** traits | **a** problems | **b** characteristics |
| **8** agreeable | **a** agree with the opinions of others | **b** relate well to other people |
| **9** be compliant | **a** obey others | **b** disobey others |

> **Exam tip:** If you have to answer multiple-choice questions, before you read the text, read the stem of each test item and underline key words.
>
> This will help you identify the part of the text that you need to read carefully in order to select the correct option A–D.
>
> Example: For Q 5 opposite, you should underline 'Adult' . When you read the text, look out for the word 'adult' (or a synonym) and read that part of the text carefully.

# Exam practice: Reading – answering multiple-choice questions

## QUESTIONS 1–5

*Look at the passage below. Choose the appropriate letters A–D to finish sentences 1–5.*

1   The term 'Four-legged Pharmaceutical' in the title refers to

    **A**  pets that cause illness            **C**  pets that need medicine

    **B**  pets that improve health         **D**  pets that give medicine

2   Asthma is probably

    **A**  a health disorder                **C**  linked to higher rates of school attendance

    **B**  a sign of good health           **D**  linked to growing up with pets at home

3   A 'risk-free' relationship is one that

    **A**  pet owners offer their pets        **C**  is not related to success or position

    **B**  you have to work hard to achieve   **D**  is linked to status but not success

4   You are less likely to suffer from asthma if

    **A**  you have contact with dogs       **C**  you stay away from dogs

    **B**  you have contact with cats        **D**  you stay away from cats

5   Adult pet owners

    **A**  do not experience benefits        **C**  experienced the same benefits as children

    **B**  experienced only limited benefits   **D**  also benefited from pet ownership

### Four-legged Pharmaceutical

Recent research suggests that pet ownership has some surprising benefits for children. The study of 256 children in three UK schools found that pets were linked to a 20% reduction in the number of days children were off sick from school. According to Dr. June McNicholas, former lecturer and world expert on human-animal interaction, owning a pet can have a positive influence on immune system functioning. She found that children who grew up in households with pets had a lower risk of developing allergies and asthma in later life.

Pets also make children happier. They are associated with improved psychological well-being, which in turn impacts positively on physical health. Physically disabled children with pets, guide dogs for example, were found to experience even greater health benefits. Pets offer psychological support and a 'risk free' relationship, a relationship not determined by achievements or status.

The study did not find significant differences between owning a cat and owning a dog, though it is possible that exposure to cats resulted in slightly better immune functioning. This confirms the results of an earlier American study which found that cats were more effective than dogs in reducing rates of asthma.

Other studies have shown that these health benefits are not limited to children. A ground-breaking Australian study found that adults who own pets had lower blood pressure and cholesterol levels. These results were confirmed by American researchers who found that the positive effect of pet ownership on blood pressure were long-lasting. Access to pets can also reduce the severity of depression among hospital patients and help ease the misery of bereavement.

# 15 Signposting expressions for writing

## Vocabulary

### Adding points:

- **furthermore**
  ADVERB **Furthermore** is used to introduce a piece of information or opinion that adds to or supports the previous one. [FORMAL]
  ▪ *Furthermore, they claim that any such interference is completely ineffective.*
  ▪ *Furthermore, even a well-timed therapy intervention may fail.*

- **moreover**
  ADVERB You use **moreover** to introduce a piece of information that adds to or supports the previous statement. [FORMAL] ▪ *The young find everything so simple. The young, moreover, see it as their duty to be happy and do their best to be so.* ▪ *A new species, it was unique to Bali – moreover, it is this island's only endemic bird.*

### Contrasting points:

- **nevertheless**
  ADVERB You use **nevertheless** when saying something that contrasts with what has just been said. [FORMAL] ▪ *Most marriages fail after between five and nine years. Nevertheless, people continue to get married.* ▪ *There had been no indication of any loss of mental faculties. His whole life had nevertheless been clouded with a series of illnesses.*

- **whereas**
  CONJUNCTION You use **whereas** to introduce a comment which contrasts with what is said in the main clause. ▪ *Pensions are linked to inflation, whereas they should be linked to the cost of living.* ▪ *Whereas the population of working age increased by 1 million between 1981 and 1986, today it is barely growing.*

- **whilst**
  CONJUNCTION **Whilst** means the same as **while**. It is used mainly in British English in formal and literary contexts. ▪ *Whilst droughts are not uncommon in many parts of the country, the coastal region remains humid throughout the year.* ▪ *Whilst every care has been taken to ensure accuracy, the publishers cannot accept legal responsibility for any problems that arise.*

### Referring to sequence:

- **former**
  PRONOUN When two people, things, or groups have just been mentioned, you can refer to the first of them as **the former**. ▪ *He writes about two series of works: the Caprichos and the Disparates. The former are a series of etchings done by Goya.* ▪ *The wife may choose the former and the husband the latter.*

- **initial**
  ADJECTIVE You use **initial** to describe something that happens at the beginning of a process. ▪ *The initial reaction has been excellent.* ▪ *The aim of this initial meeting is to clarify the issues.*

- **latter**
  PRONOUN When two people, things, or groups have just been mentioned, you can refer to the second of them as **the latter**.

• *At school, he enjoyed football and boxing; the latter remained a lifelong habit.* • *Without hesitation they chose the latter.*

• **prior**
ADJECTIVE You use **prior** to indicate that something has already happened, or must happen, before another event takes place. • *Prior knowledge of the program is not essential.* • *For the prior year, they reported net income of $1.1 million.*
PHRASE If something happens **prior to** a particular time or event, it happens before that time or event. [FORMAL] • *Prior to his Japan trip, he went to New York.* • *This is the preliminary investigation prior to the official inquiry.*

• **respectively**
ADVERB **Respectively** means in the same order as the items that you have just mentioned. • *Their sons, Ben and Jonathan, were three and six respectively.* • *Obesity and high blood pressure occurred in 16 per cent and 14 per cent of Australian adults, respectively.*

• **subsequent**
ADJECTIVE You use **subsequent** to describe something that happened or existed after the time or event that has just been referred to. [FORMAL] • *the increase of population in subsequent years* • *Those concerns were overshadowed by subsequent events.*

## Generalizing:

• **on balance**
PHRASE You can say on balance to indicate that you are stating an opinion after considering all the relevant facts or arguments. • *On balance he agreed with Christine.*

• **overall**
ADVERB You use **overall** to indicate that you are talking about a situation in general or about the whole of something. • *The review omitted some studies. Overall, however, the evidence was persuasive.* • *The college has few ways to assess the quality of education overall.*

## Expressing consequence and concluding:

• **hence**
ADVERB You use **hence** to indicate that the statement you are about to make is a consequence of what you have just said. [FORMAL] • *The trade imbalance is likely to rise again in 1990. Hence a new set of policy actions will be required soon.* • *European music happens to use a scale of eight notes, hence the use of the term octave.*

• **thus**
ADVERB You use **thus** to show that what you are about to mention is the result or consequence of something else that you have just mentioned. [FORMAL] • *Even in a highly skilled workforce some people will be more capable and thus better paid than others.* • *women's access to the basic means of production and thus to political power*

## Practice exercises

1   Match the beginning of each sentence 1–6 with the most appropriate ending a–f.

| | | | |
|---|---|---|---|
| **1** | Employment opportunities for graduates have declined; _____ | **a** | prior to the granting of planning permission. |
| **2** | He explained the terms 'biosphere' and 'ecosystem'; the former refers to the atmosphere, water and land where life occurs and _____ | **b** | moreover, the poorest ten per cent should be given immediate assistance. |

| | | | |
|---|---|---|---|
| **3** | Steps should be taken to raise the living standards of all families living below the poverty line; _____ | **c** | whilst in most industrialised countries, the majority of pupils study mathematics until the age of 18. |
| **4** | In the United Kingdom, only 15 per cent of pupils pursue the subject beyond the age of 16, _____ | **d** | thus women suffer disproportionately when there are cuts in government expenditure. |
| **5** | There must be a thorough assessment of the environmental impact of the new development _____ | **e** | nevertheless, young people continue to aspire to a university education. ____ |
| **6** | A higher proportion of women work in the public sector; _____ | **f** | the latter refers to the interaction between living things and their environment. |

**2**   For each sentence 1–6 above, write a letter a–e indicating whether a point has been:

  **a**   added

  **b**   contrasted

  **c**   sequenced (put in order)

  **d**   expressed as a consequence

---

**Exam tip:** Learn how linking words are used – notice the grammar and punctuation of the example sentences below.

The adverbs *furthermore, moreover, nevertheless, thus* and *hence* link two sentences or clauses.

> *Nursing homes are very costly. <u>Moreover</u>, they often fail to provide adequate levels of care. Grown-up children frequently settle in other cities; <u>hence</u>, the elderly often find themselves without family nearby.*

Use *nevertheless,* when you want to emphasize that the idea in the second sentence or clause is contrary to what the reader would expect from the first.

> *He knew he had lost the race. <u>Nevertheless</u>, he pressed on until the finish line.*

The conjunctions *whereas and whilst* are used to contrast information within a sentence.

> *Dogs like company, <u>whereas</u> most cats prefer to be on their own.*

---

**3**   For each sentence 1–6, underline the word in italics that can be used to complete the sentence.

  **1**   He worked casually for several years *prior/initial* to receiving a proper job contract.

  **2**   Many independent film makers achieve critical success; *whilst/nevertheless* they often find it difficult to raise funds for future projects.

  **3**   At first we decided that *hence/on balance,* starting a business would be a worthwhile experience.

  **4**   His *subsequent/respectively* book was not as good as his first.

  **5**   The west of the county has a tropical climate, *whereas/nevertheless* the east is quite arid.

  **6**   Ireland and Greece joined the European Union in 1973 and 1981 *latter/respectively.*

**Exam tip:** Learn the different types of sequencing words and how they are used.
*Former, initial, prior, latter* and *subsequent* are adjectives and can be used to modify nouns.
Examples: *My former wife is in town.   Jane's initial response to the news was quite positive.*

*Former* and *latter* are also pronouns which can be used in place of nouns mentioned previously.
Example: *Jim saw both cheetahs and lions. He was able to photograph the former but not the latter.*

*Respectively* is an adverb which usually comes at the end of a clause.
Example: *For English and mathematics, he was awarded an A and a B respectively.*

*Prior to* is a formal phrase that can be used in place of the preposition 'before'.
Example: *The patient had been well prior to the operation.*

4  **Complete the passage with words from this unit. For some gaps, there may be more than one possible answer.**

Studying abroad has become increasingly challenging over the last year or two. Visa regulations have become more complex and the cost of travelling abroad has increased substantially. (1) ＿＿＿＿＿＿, record numbers of students have applied for a place at a university overseas. When international students first arrive in the new country, their (2) ＿＿＿＿＿＿ impression is often favourable. However, their (3) ＿＿＿＿＿＿ impressions can be less so, as they struggle to adapt. International students need time to adjust to the new study environment; (4) ＿＿＿＿＿＿, they need help with that process. Decisions about how best to help international students will depend on their needs. Undergraduate and postgraduate students are very different; the (5) ＿＿＿＿＿＿ may need an introduction to essay writing; the latter more advanced training in critical thinking skills. The student's subject is also a factor to be born in mind. Good numeracy skills are needed for engineering for example, (6) ＿＿＿＿＿＿ good literacy skills are needed for courses such as law.

## Exam practice: Writing Task 2

The essay introduction below has been written in response to the Task 2 question:

> *Increasing numbers of students are choosing to study abroad. To what extent does this trend benefit the students themselves and the countries involved? What are the drawbacks?*

**Rewrite the introduction by replacing the words in bold with signposting words from this unit. Make any necessary changes to punctuation. Then complete the essay in your own words using appropriate signposting expressions where necessary.**

**Write at least 250 words in total.**
Studying abroad has become increasingly common in the last few years, especially for young people from countries such as China and India.  Many students and their families clearly consider the experience worth the sacrifices involved. **Students** often give up friendships when they move abroad; **families** often use their life savings. **And** many governments are willing to invest huge sums of money in sponsoring their young people to study in universities overseas. However, this trend has drawbacks as well as benefits for those concerned.

# 16 Adverbs

## Vocabulary

- **absolutely**
  1 ADVERB **Absolutely** means totally and completely. ▪ *Jill is absolutely right.* ▪ *I absolutely refuse to do it.* ▪ *There is absolutely no difference!*
  2 ADVERB Some people say **absolutely** as an emphatic way of saying yes or of agreeing with someone. They say **absolutely not** as an emphatic way of saying no. ▪ *'It's worrying, isn't it?' – 'Absolutely.'*

- **approximately**
  ADVERB You use **approximately** to show that a number or amount is not exact or accurate. ▪ *Approximately $150 million is to be spent on improvements.* ▪ *Each session lasted approximately 30 to 40 minutes.*

- **comparatively**
  ADVERB You use **comparatively** when you are contrasting two or more things or people. ▪ *a comparatively small nation* ▪ *children who find it comparatively easy to make and keep friends*

- **ideally**
  ADVERB  If you say that **ideally** a particular thing should happen or be done, you mean that this is what would be best, but you know that this may not be possible or practical. ▪ *People should, ideally, eat much less fat.* ▪ *The restructuring ideally needs to be completed this year.*

- **indefinitely**
  ADVERB If a situation will continue **indefinitely**, it will continue for ever or until someone decides to change it or end it. ▪ *The visit has now been postponed indefinitely.* ▪ *The school has been closed indefinitely.*

- **inevitably**
  ADVERB If something will **inevitably** happen, it is certain to happen and cannot be prevented or avoided. ▪ *Technological changes will inevitably lead to unemployment.* ▪ *Inevitably, the proposal is running into difficulties.*

- **interestingly**
  ADVERB You use **interestingly** to introduce a piece of information that you think is interesting or unexpected. ▪ *Interestingly enough, a few weeks later, he remarried.*

- **necessarily**
  ADVERB If you say that something is **not necessarily** the case, you mean that it may not be the case or is not always the case. ▪ *A higher fee does not necessarily mean a better course.*

- **particularly**
  ADVERB **Particularly** means more than usual or more than other things. ▪ *Progress has been particularly disappointing.* ▪ *I was not particularly interested in the conversation.*

- **presumably**
  ADVERB If you say that something is **presumably** the case, you mean that you think it is very likely to be the case, although you are not certain. ▪ *He had gone to the reception desk, presumably to check out.*

- **provisionally**
  ADVERB **Provisionally** means arranged or appointed for the present, with the possibility of being changed in the future. ▪ *The seven republics had provisionally agreed*

to the new relationship on November 14th.
▪ *A meeting is provisionally scheduled for early next week.*

- **relatively**
  ADVERB **Relatively** means to a certain degree, especially when compared with other things of the same kind. ▪ *The sums needed are relatively small.* ▪ *Such an explanation makes it relatively easy for a child to absorb metaphysical information.*

- **supposedly**
  ADVERB Something that is **supposedly** true, is said to be true by some people. ▪ *He was supposedly a tough man to work for.* ▪ *They*

supposedly agreed to leave their homes and property and never return.

- **surprisingly**
  ADVERB You use **surprisingly** to introduce a piece of information that you think is unexpected or unusual. ▪ *He did surprisingly well in the election last year.* ▪ *Surprisingly, he did as she asked.*

- **undoubtedly**
  ADVERB If something is **undoubtedly** true, it is certainly so. ▪ *Undoubtedly, political and economic factors have played their part.* ▪ *These sort of statistics are undoubtedly alarming.* ▪ *It is undoubtedly true that harder times are on the way.*

## Practice exercises

**1**   **Underline the seven adverbs in the dialogue below.**

| | |
|---|---|
| Examiner: | Tell me about the house or flat you live in. |
| Candidate: | I'm living in my aunt's flat at the moment. I've provisionally arranged to stay there until I complete my studies. It's a relatively small flat, approximately 70 square metres, and on the top floor of a four-storey building. |
| Examiner: | How do you feel about living there? |
| Candidate: | Ideally, I'd like a bigger flat, but it'll do for now.  I wouldn't want to stay there indefinitely as it's a long commute to my university. |
| Examiner: | Is the decoration or appearance of the place you live important to you? |
| Candidate: | Not particularly. As long as it's clean and comfortable, I'm happy. |
| Examiner: | When choosing things for your flat, is the appearance of an object more important to you than how well it works? |
| Candidate: | Not necessarily. I prefer objects that are well designed, which to me, means things that are both  functional and attractive. |

**2**   **Match the adverbs and expressions 1–7 below with the adverbs you underlined in Exercise 1.**

   **1**   especially
   **2**   preferably
   **3**   temporarily/for the time being
   **4**   without a fixed time limit
   **5**   always/definitely
   **6**   roughly
   **7**   comparatively

**3** For each sentence 1–7 replace the expression in italics with the most appropriate adverb a–g. Listen to Track 28 to check your answers.

**28**

| | | | |
|---|---|---|---|
| **a** | absolutely | **e** | supposedly |
| **b** | inevitably | **f** | surprisingly |
| **c** | interestingly | **g** | undoubtedly |
| **d** | presumably | | |

**1** *I didn't expect this* - the prime minister has been elected for a second term.

**2** *I was intrigued that* more young people voted in this election than in the previous one.

**3** *Yes, of course!* I'd love to return to Africa some day.

**4** *People claim that* travel broadens the mind.

**5** *I'm sure that* cooking with natural ingredients is better for your health.

**6** *We cannot avoid the fact that* the cost of fuel will rise.

**7** *I assume* fewer people will travel by car if petrol becomes too expensive.

**4** Listen to words 1–6 below on Track 29. Circle the vowel which is stressed and underline any vowels pronounced as a schwa. Say the words.

**29**

| | | | |
|---|---|---|---|
| **1** | absolutely | **4** | presumably |
| **2** | necessarily | **5** | supposedly |
| **3** | particularly | **6** | surprisingly |

**5** Listen to the examiner's questions in Exercise 1 on Track 30, pausing the CD after each question. Answer the questions in your own words using adverbs where appropriate.

**30**

# Exam practice: Speaking Part 1

**Exam tip:** Using attitude markers such as *surprisingly*, *interestingly*, and *inevitably* can make your responses more interesting. However, if you overuse them or use them inappropriately you will not sound natural.

Notice how proficient speakers use them and in what contexts.

Avoid using them in every sentence.

31

You are going to practise Part 1 of the IELTS Speaking exam: introduction and interview.

You will hear the examiner introduce herself, ask you to confirm your identity, and ask you questions on a variety of topics.

This part of the exam takes 4–5 minutes.

As you do this practice exercise, pause the CD after each question so that you can answer.

You may want to record yourself, assess your performance, and try again.

Sample answers to the questions are in the Answer key on page 108.

# 17 Words for problems and solutions

Nouns and verbs for problems and solutions | Recognizing connotation | Recognizing collocations

## Vocabulary

### Nouns for problems:

- **complication (complications)**
  NOUN A **complication** is a problem or difficulty that makes a situation harder to deal with. ▪ *The age difference was a complication to the relationship.* ▪ *An added complication is the growing concern for the environment.*

- **crisis (crises)**
  NOUN A **crisis** is a situation in which something or someone is affected by one or more very serious problems. ▪ *Natural disasters have obviously contributed to the continent's economic crisis.* ▪ *children's illnesses or other family crises* ▪ *someone to turn to in moments of crisis*

- **dilemma (dilemmas)**
  NOUN A **dilemma** is a difficult situation in which you have to choose between two or more alternatives. ▪ *Many Muslim women face the terrible dilemma of having to choose between employment and their Islamic garb.* ▪ *The issue raises a moral dilemma.*

- **predicament (predicaments)**
  NOUN If you are in a **predicament**, you are in an unpleasant situation that is difficult to get out of. ▪ *The decision will leave her in a peculiar predicament.* ▪ *The army was at last realizing its predicament.*

### Verbs associated with problems:

- **damage (damages, damaging, damaged)**
  VERB To **damage** something means to cause it to become less good, pleasant, or successful. ▪ *Jackson doesn't want to damage his reputation as a political personality.* ▪ *He warned that the action was damaging the economy.*

- **deteriorate (deteriorates, deteriorating, deteriorated)**
  VERB If something **deteriorates**, it becomes worse in some way. ▪ [+ *into*] *There are fears that the situation might deteriorate into full-scale war.* ▪ [V-ing] *Surface transport has become less and less viable with deteriorating road conditions.* ▪ *Relations between the two countries steadily deteriorated.*

### Verbs associated with solutions:

- **address (addresses, addressing, addressed)**
  VERB If you **address** a problem or task, you try to understand it or deal with it. ▪ *Mr King sought to address those fears when he spoke at the meeting.* ▪ *US policy has failed to adequately address this problem.*

- **alleviate (alleviates, alleviating, alleviated)**
  VERB If you **alleviate** pain suffering or an unpleasant condition, you make it less intense or severe. [FORMAL] ▪ *Nowadays a great deal can be done to alleviate back pain.*

■ *Part of his job is to develop programs to alleviate homelessness.*

- **approach (approaches, approaching, approached)**
VERB When you **approach** a task, problem, or situation in a particular way, you deal with it or think about it in that way. ■ *The Bank has approached the issue in a practical way.* ■ *Employers are interested in how you approach problems.*

- **eradicate (eradicates, eradicating, eradicated)**
VERB To **eradicate** something means to get rid of it completely. [FORMAL] ■ *They are already battling to eradicate illnesses such as malaria and tetanus.* ■ *[+ in] Vaccination has virtually eradicated anthrax in the developed world.* ■ *a campaign that genuinely sought to eradicate poverty*

- **intervene (intervenes, intervening, intervened)**
VERB If you **intervene in** a situation, you become involved in it and try to change it. ■ *The situation calmed down when police intervened.* ■ *[+ in] The Government is doing nothing to intervene in the crisis.*

- **react (reacts, reacting, reacted)**
VERB When you **react to** something that has happened to you, you behave in a particular way because of it. ■ *[+ to] They reacted violently to the news.* ■ *It's natural to react with disbelief if your child is accused of bullying.*

- **repair (repairs, repairing, repaired)**
VERB If you **repair** something that has been damaged or is not working properly, you mend it. ■ *A woman drove her car to the garage to have it repaired.* ■ *The roof will be repaired to ensure the house is wind-proof.*

- **resolve (resolves, resolving, resolved)**
VERB To **resolve** a problem, argument, or difficulty means to find a solution to it. [FORMAL] ■ *We must find a way to resolve these problems before it's too late.* ■ *They hoped the crisis could be resolved peacefully.*

- **tackle (tackles, tackling, tackled)**
VERB If you **tackle** a difficult problem or task, you deal with it in a very determined or efficient way. ■ *The first reason to tackle these problems is to save children's lives.* ■ *the government's latest scheme to tackle crime.*

## Practice exercises

1   Match the words a–d with the situations 1–4.

| a complication | b crisis | c dilemma | d predicament |
|---|---|---|---|

1   I can't decide whether to go on holiday with my best friend or attend my aunt's wedding. Whatever I decide, someone's going to be very disappointed. _____

2   My house was set alight at the weekend and everything I own has been destroyed! _____

3   They're very much in love, but he lives in San Francisco, and she lives in London. That certainly makes things difficult. _____

4   My passport's expired and I've got to send it off to be renewed. But I need to present my passport to the examiner in order to sit the test next week. What an impossible situation! _____

🎧 **2**
32

Listen to each speaker 1–5 describe a problem. Complete each sentence 1–5 with the most appropriate word a–e.

**a** crisis
**b** damage
**c** deterioration

**d** dilemma
**e** predicament

1 The speaker is angry about _____ to her car.
2 The speaker is concerned about the _____ in her grandmother's health.
3 The speaker complains about a _____ that he's in.
4 The speaker is experiencing a _____ and needs help.
5 The speaker is struggling with a _____.

🎧 **3**
33

For each sentence 1–5 underline the word in italics that best collocates with the word in bold. Listen and check your answers.

1 Don't worry. The **damage** to your car can be easily *resolved/repaired*.
2 I'm sure you'd like to do more to *intervene in/alleviate* her **suffering**.
3 If you speak to your manager, she may be able to *resolve/react to* your **predicament**.
4 I'll be right over! That's not a **crisis** you should *tackle/eradicate* on your own.
5 You're never going to *repair/resolve* that **dilemma** until you decide what you really want.

**4** For each sentence 1–6 underline the word in italics which has the more moderate meaning.

1 If you make the wrong choice, you could *damage/destroy* your career.
2 Management have promised to *solve/address* the problem of falling productivity.
3 The government has pledged to *tackle/eradicate* child poverty by 2025.
4 Women are often faced with the *question/dilemma* of how to balance family and work commitments.
5 There's been a *crisis/complication* with the building work; it's nothing too serious, but I'm afraid it's put us behind schedule by a few days.
6 Employing nurses from overseas may *alleviate/resolve* the skills shortage in the short term, but more needs to be done for the longer term.

> **Exam tip:** For questions in the Listening exam which require you to write the answer:
> Use only words that you hear in the recording.
> Make sure that you spell the words correctly.

**5**  Underline and correct the nine words which have been misspelled in the paragraph below.

Culture shock can be defined as the difficulty people experience when ajusting to a new culture that is significantly diffrent from their own. There are no fixed symptoms associated with culture shock as each individual reacts to the experience in his or her own way. However, the shock of moving to a foriegn country is often seen as consisting of distinct phases. There is often an initial period of enthusiasm and positive feeling, sometimes refered to as a 'honeymoon phase', followed by a period of growing frustration and anxiety. Over time, the newcomer enters a third phase, a period of ajustment, during which new coping skills are developed. Finally, there is a period of acceptance – the individual can operate in the new enviroment with ease.

There is no set way of aproaching the problem of culture shock. Evidence suggests that each person learns to cope with the transition in their own way. However, the unpleasant symptoms associated with the more difficult phases can be aleviated by a few simple measures: rest, good nutrition, and plenty of social contact.

## Exam practice: Listening – short-answer questions

**Exam tip:** For any question which requires you to write an answer, follow the instructions exactly.

If the instructions tell you to write no more than three words, you can write one, two or three words.

If you have to write more than three words to answer the question, you have probably chosen the wrong information.

### QUESTIONS 1–5

*Answer the questions below. Write NO MORE THAN THREE WORDS AND/OR A NUMBER for each answer.*

**1**  Kerry Wilson is a member of which team?

**2**  If students have a problem opening a bank account, what should they obtain from the Language Centre?

**3**  Disputes with landlords can arise in relation to what type of problem?

**4**  If a student has a disagreement with a landlord, what can members of the welfare team do?

**5**  In case of a crisis, where can students find the emergency telephone number?

# 18 Words for talking about ideas

## Vocabulary

### Nouns for ideas:

- **concept (concepts)**
  NOUN A **concept** is an idea or abstract principle. ▪ [+ of] *She added that the concept of arranged marriages is misunderstood in the west.* ▪ *basic legal concepts*

- **conjecture (conjectures)**
  NOUN A **conjecture** is a conclusion that is based on information that is not certain or complete. [FORMAL] ▪ *That was a conjecture, not a fact.* ▪ *Ozone creation is a very large-scale natural process and the importance of humangenerated CFCs in reducing it is largely a matter of conjecture.*

- **consensus**
  NOUN A **consensus** is general agreement among a group of people. ▪ [+ amongst] *The consensus amongst the world's scientists is that the world is likely to warm up over the next few decades.* ▪ [+ on] *So far, the Australians have been unable to come to a uniform consensus on the issue.*

- **dogma (dogmas)**
  NOUN If you refer to a belief or a system of beliefs as a **dogma**, you disapprove of it because people are expected to accept that it is true, without questioning it. ▪ *Their political dogma has blinded them to the real needs of the country.* ▪ *He stands for freeing the country from the grip of dogma.*

- **framework (frameworks)**
  NOUN A **framework** is a particular set of rules, ideas, or beliefs which you use in order to deal with problems or to decide what to do. ▪ [+ for] *The purpose of the chapter is to provide a framework for thinking about why exchange rates change.* ▪ *Doctors need a clear legal framework to be able to deal with difficult clinical decisions.*

- **ideology (ideologies)**
  NOUN An **ideology** is a set of beliefs, especially the political beliefs on which people, parties, or countries base their actions. ▪ [+ of] *Fifteen years after the president embraced the ideology of privatization, the people were worse off than ever.* ▪ *North Carolina more than any other southern state, is the home of two disparate, yet equally powerful, political ideologies.*

- **model (models)**
  NOUN A **model** of a system or process is a theoretical description that can help you understand how the system or process works, or how it might work. [FORMAL] ▪ [+ of] *Darwin eventually put forward a model of biological evolution.*

- **perspective (perspectives)**
  NOUN A particular **perspective** is a particular way of thinking about something, especially one that is influenced by your beliefs or experiences. ▪ [+ on] *two different perspectives on the nature of adolescent development* ▪ [+ of] *Most literature on the subject of immigrants in France has been written from the perspective of the French themselves.* ▪ *I would like to offer a historical perspective.*

- **stance (stances)**
  NOUN Your **stance** on a particular matter is
  your attitude to it. ▪ [+ *on*] *The Congress had
  agreed to reconsider its stance on the armed
  struggle.* ▪ *They have maintained a consistently
  neutral stance.* ▪ [+ *towards*] *His stance
  towards the story is quite similar to ours.*

### Adjectives for describing ideas:

- **ambiguous**
  ADJECTIVE If you describe something as
  **ambiguous**, you mean that it is unclear or
  confusing because it can be understood in
  more than one way. ▪ *This agreement is very
  ambiguous and open to various interpretations.*
  ▪ *The Foreign Secretary's remarks clarify an
  ambiguous statement issued earlier this week.*

- **biased**
  ADJECTIVE If someone is **biased**, they prefer
  one group of people to another and behave
  unfairly as a result. ▪ [+ *against*] *He seemed
  a bit biased against women in my opinion.*
  ▪ [+ *towards*] *University funding was
  tremendously biased towards scientists.*
  ▪ *examples of inaccurate and biased reporting*

- **compelling**
  ADJECTIVE A **compelling** argument or
  reason is one that convinces you that

something is true or that something should
be done. ▪ *Forensic evidence makes a suicide
verdict the most compelling answer to the
mystery of his death.* ▪ *The evidence was
so compelling that the government did not
have to force this change; it was willingly
accepted.*

- **credible**
  ADJECTIVE **Credible** means able to be trusted
  or believed. ▪ [+ *to*] *BaronessThatcher's
  claims seem credible to many.* ▪ *But in order to
  maintain a credible threat of intervention, we
  have to maintain a credible alliance.*

- **flawed**
  ADJECTIVE Something that is **flawed** has
  a mark, fault, or mistake in it. ▪ *the unique
  beauty of a flawed object* ▪ *These tests were
  so seriously flawed as to render the results
  meaningless.* ▪ *The problem is the original
  forecast was based on flawed assumptions.*

- **valid**
  ADJECTIVE A **valid** argument, comment, or
  idea is based on sensible reasoning. ▪ *They put
  forward many valid reasons for not exporting.*
  ▪ *Some of these arguments are valid.* ▪ *This
  is a perfectly valid approach, but it has its
  drawbacks.*

## Practice exercises

1   Complete each sentence 1–8 with the most appropriate word a–h.

| a concept | c consensus | e framework | g perspective |
|-----------|-------------|-------------|---------------|
| b conjecture | d dogma | f ideology | h stance |

1   The religious _____ of the time prevented these innovative ideas from gaining
    wider acceptance.

2   The government is reconsidering its _____ on welfare reform and now appears to
    more or less in agreement with the main opposition party.

3   The development of international law is interesting when viewed from a historical
    _____.

4   We dismissed his accusation of theft because it was based on _____ rather than fact.

5   The prime minister was criticized for basing his approach to economic problems on
    political _____ rather than on a reasonable assessment of the situation.

6   Despite intense negotiation, the committee was unable to reach a _____.

7   The time-space continuum is a difficult _____ to grasp unless you are a physicist.

8   Hofstede developed an interesting _____ for comparing cultures.

**2** Underline the adjectives that have a positive meaning. Circle those which have a negative meaning.

**1** ambiguous      **3** compelling      **5** flawed

**2** biased      **4** credible      **6** valid

**3** Match the beginning of each sentence 1–4 with the most appropriate ending a–d.

**1** The former dictator was convicted of war crimes... _____

**a** ...because it failed to consider the objections of local residents.

**2** He is unlikely to win the debate... _____

**b** ...as no one was able to offer a credible alternative.

**3** I thought the planning committee's stance was biased in favour of property developers... _____

**c** ...unless he can put forward a valid argument.

**4** The negotiators decided to stick with the original framework for peace... _____

**d** ...as the evidence against him was compelling.

**4** Complete the table below with the missing parts of speech.

| noun | _____ | _____ | concept | _____ | dogma | _____ |
|---|---|---|---|---|---|---|
| adjective | ambiguous | biased | _____ | credible | _____ | valid |

> **Exam tip:** In the IELTS Reading exam you may have to complete gaps in a summary with words from a reading passage. Recognizing which part of speech is required in a gap can help you do this.
>
> Example: *He won the argument because he was able to present the most _____ evidence.*
>
> In this sentence the gap comes before a noun so it is likely to require an adjective.
>
> *He won the argument because he was able to present the most **credible** evidence.*

**5** Complete the summary with words from the text underneath. Use each word once only.

Many educators have tried to devise a (1) _____ for understanding the reading process. Some maintain that readers use a bottom-up approach. Others have questioned the (2) _____ of this view, arguing instead that readers use a 'top-down' strategy based on their understanding of the reading passage context. However, this (3) _____ also has (4) _____.

## The reading process

Educators have made numerous attempts to develop a framework for making sense of what goes on in the mind of the reader in the process of reading a text. Some believe that readers build up an understanding of a text from the 'bottom-up': that is, they decode individual words first, then sentences, then paragraphs and so on. Critics have cast doubt on the validity of this model by pointing out, for example, that readers can often understand texts which have words missing.

Those who adopt an alternative stance maintain that readers employ a 'top-down' approach to reading. They believe that readers use their understanding of the overall context of the reading passage to work out the meaning of individual words, phrases and sentences. However, flaws have also been identified in this perspective. It is obvious, for example, that it would be impossible for readers to read a text written in a language completely unknown to them, however much they knew about the context.

# Exam practice: Reading – completing a summary – matching sentence endings

## QUESTIONS 1–6

*Complete the summary below with words from the reading passage underneath. Use NO MORE THAN THREE WORDS for each answer.*

### Summary

For many years, (1) _____ have tried to define the concept of humour but failed to reach a (2) _____. Although numerous (3) _____ of humour have been identified, three main categories are commonly recognized: superiority, (4) _____. Proponents of the superiority model believe that people see humour in the (5) _____ of others. However, this interpretation is not always (6) _____.

### What is humour?

We all recognize it when we see it, but do we really know what it is? For over 2500 years, philosophers and psychologists have tried to answer this question; however, there has been little consensus to date over what, in essence, constitutes humour. Indeed, some scholars have identified as many as 100 distinct theories of humour in the literature on the subject.

The standard analysis classifies theories of humour into three broad categories: superiority, relief and incongruity. The superiority theory can be traced back to the ancient Greek philosophers Aristotle and Plato, who maintained that we laugh at the misfortune or inferiority of others: the ugly, the ill-educated, and the uncouth. According to this framework, our sense of superiority brings about a feeling of joy or pleasure. Whilst this may explain some instances of humour, it is clearly not valid in every case: we can often feel superior to something, an insect for example, without finding the situation funny.

Relief theorists, on the other hand, propose a 'tension-release' model to the problem of humour. Proponents of this approach see laughter as a release of nervous or pent-up energy. The psychoanalyst Sigmund Freud, for example, noted that jokes often touch on taboo subjects such as infidelity or death. He believed that laughter is a release of psychic energy that would normally be used to suppress awareness of uncomfortable subjects. However, this theory too has its flaws. Some critics have pointed out that the failure to distinguish between laughter (a physical response) and humour (a concept relating to thought or feeling) has resulted in unhelpful ambiguity.

This brings us to the third category: incongruity theories of humour. According to this framework, humour occurs when there is a sudden resolution of a mismatch between expectation and reality. Puns, jokes which play on the double meaning of words, are a good illustration of this view. For example, 'I needed a password eight characters long so I picked Snow White and the Seven Dwarves' plays on the dual meaning of the word 'character'. In the first part of the sentence the listener develops the expectation that 'characters' refers to letters of the alphabet. The humorous twist occurs when the teller reveals that he has in fact chosen as his password characters (fictional people) from a well-known animated film. While incongruity theories of humour are generally seen as having the greatest credibility, they too have their critics. Experience tells us that some incongruities – finding a shoe in your refrigerator, for example – may simply be experienced as perplexing or uncomfortable.

What can one conclude from this? Perhaps only that whilst each of these approaches can explain some instances of humour, no single one has captured every aspect of this most elusive quality.

# 19 Emphasis and understatement

## Vocabulary

### Adjectives describing quantity and degree:

- **abundant**
  ADJECTIVE Something that is **abundant** is present in large quantities. ▪ *There is an abundant supply of cheap labour.* ▪ *Birds are abundant in the tall vegetation.* ▪ *Hydrogen is the most abundant element in the universe.*

- **ample**
  ADJECTIVE If there is an **ample** amount of something, there is enough of it and usually some extra. ▪ *There'll be ample opportunity to relax, swim and soak up some sun.* ▪ *There were ample supplies of vegetables and fruit as well.*

- **marked**
  ADJECTIVE A **marked** change or difference is very obvious and easily noticed. ▪ *There has been a marked increase in crimes against property.* ▪ *He was a man of austere habits, in marked contrast to his more flamboyant wife.* ▪ *The trends since the 1950s have become even more marked.*

- **modest**
  ADJECTIVE You use **modest** to describe something such as an amount, rate or improvement which is fairly small. ▪ *Unemployment rose to the still modest rate of 0.7%.* ▪ *The democratic reforms have been modest.*

- **negligible**
  ADJECTIVE An amount or effect that is **negligible** is so small that it is not worth considering or worrying about. ▪ *The pay that the soldiers received was negligible.* ▪ *Senior managers are convinced that the strike will have a negligible impact.* ▪ *cut down to negligible proportions*

- **vast**
  ADJECTIVE Something that is **vast** is extremely large. ▪ *The farmers own vast stretches of land.* ▪ *The vast majority of the eggs will be cracked.*

### Adjectives describing degree of certainty:

- **definitive**
  ADJECTIVE Something that is **definitive** provides a firm conclusion that cannot be questioned. ▪ *The study population was too small to reach any definitive conclusions.* ▪ *There is no definitive test as yet for the condition.*

- **liable**
  PHRASE When something **is liable to** happen, it is very likely to happen. ▪ *Only a small minority of the mentally ill are liable to harm themselves or others.* ▪ *He is liable to change his mind quite rapidly.*

- **tentative**
  ADJECTIVE **Tentative** agreements, plans, or arrangements are not definite or certain, but have been made as a first step. ▪ *Political leaders have reached a tentative agreement to hold a preparatory conference next month.* ▪ *Such theories are still very tentative.* ▪ *The study was adequate to permit at least tentative conclusions.*

- **undisputed**
  ADJECTIVE If you describe a fact or an opinion as **undisputed**, you are trying to persuade someone that it is generally accepted as true or correct. ▪ *the undisputed fact that he had broken the law* ▪ *his undisputed genius*

## Adverbs describing quantity and degree:

- **marginally**
  ADVERB **Marginally** means to only a small extent. ▪ *Sales last year were marginally higher than in 1991.* ▪ *The Christian Democrats did marginally worse than expected.* ▪ *These cameras have increased only marginally in value over the past decade.*

- **seldom**
  ADVERB If something **seldom** happens, it happens only occasionally. ▪ *They seldom speak.* ▪ *Hypertension can be controlled but seldom cured.* ▪ *The fines were seldom sufficient to force any permanent change.*

## Adverbs describing degree of certainty:

- **ostensibly**
  ADVERB If something is **ostensibly** true, it seems to be true, but you or other people have doubts about it. ▪ *ostensibly independent organisations*

- **reportedly**
  ADVERB If you say that something is **reportedly** true, you mean that someone has said that it is true, but you have no direct evidence of it. [FORMAL] ▪ *More than two hundred people have reportedly been killed in the past week's fighting.* ▪ *Now Moscow has reportedly agreed that the sale can go ahead.* ▪ *General Breymann had been shot dead, reportedly by one of his own men.*

- **seemingly**
  ADVERB You use **seemingly** when you want to say that something seems to be true. ▪ *He moved to Spain, seemingly to enjoy a slower style of life.*

# Practice exercises

> **Exam tip:** In the IELTS Writing exam you can use words such as *vast* and *marginally* to present facts, figures or trends effectively.
>
> Some adjectives and adverbs convey the idea of 'big', 'very' or 'a lot'.
>
> Example: <u>*Vast*</u> *amounts of money have been spent on IT projects that have proved unworkable.*
>
> Other adjectives and adverbs convey the idea of 'small' or 'a little'.
>
> Example: *The percentage of students studying science and engineering was* <u>*marginally*</u> *higher last year than it has been in the previous ten years.*

1  **For each sentence 1–5 circle the words in bold which are similar in meaning to *big* or *a lot of*. Underline the words in bold which are similar in meaning to *small*.**

　**1**  There is **abundant** evidence that wearing a seatbelt reduces the risk of serious injury from automobile accidents.

　**2**  There was a **negligible** rise in unemployment in the last quarter.

　**3**  We have **ample** proof that the stolen money is being held in an off-shore account.

　**4**  There is a **marked** difference between urban and rural areas in terms of job losses.

　**5**  There was a **modest** increase in exam pass rates last year.

**2** **For each sentence 1–5 circle the word or expression in italics that makes the stronger claim.**

**1** Based on the evidence available to date, we have come to the *tentative/definitive* conclusion that smaller class sizes improved pupils' educational attainment.

**2** The evidence that smoking increases the risk of lung cancer is *undisputed/strong.*

**3** It has been *reported/confirmed* that the royal wedding will take place in August.

**4** Heavily indebted companies *will/are liable to* fail in the current economic climate.

**5** The workers were *seemingly/known to be* contented with the changes to their working conditions.

**3** **For each sentence 1–6, cross out the word a–c which does not collocate with the word in bold.**

**1** Psychologists have come to a/the _____ **conclusion** that children of working mothers are not educationally disadvantaged.

    **a** tentative           **b** ample           **c** definitive

**2** There is _____ **evidence** that genetically engineered foods are safe to eat.

    **a** abundant          **b** ample           **c** marked

**3** Recent government reforms had a/an _____ **effect** on the budget deficit.

    **a** abundant          **b** negligible       **c** modest

**4** The graph shows that there has been a/an _____ **increase** in the average daily consumption of fresh fruit and vegetables.

    **a** marked           **b** modest          **c** abundant

**5** Negotiators for the two countries have reached a _____ **agreement** on how to resolve the border dispute.

    **a** tentative           **b** definitive       **c** vast

**6** The rebels have obtained _____ **supplies** of weapons.

    **a** vast               **b** abundant       **c** marked

**4** **For each sentence 1–6 replace the word or expression in bold with one of the key words from this unit.**

**1** If my boss comes under any more pressure, she's **likely** to explode.

**2** Because of more effective policing, there has been a **noticeable** decrease in youth crime.

**3** Job prospects for graduates have improved **slightly** over the last six months.

**4** People who gamble **rarely** win more than they lose.

**5** No one has been able to give a **conclusive** answer to the question of why some people seem to be consistently luckier than others.

# Exam practice: Writing Task 1

Using adjectives and adverbs of quantity and degree complete the report below.

*The graph below shows the number of hours per day on average that children spent watching television. The graph covers the period between 1950 and 2010.*

*Summarize the information by selecting and reporting the main features, and make comparisons where relevant.*

**Write at least 150 words.**

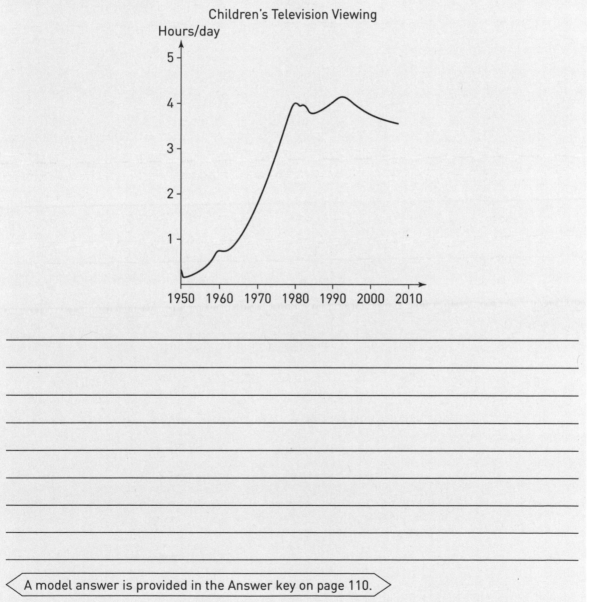

Children's Television Viewing

_____

_____

_____

_____

_____

_____

_____

_____

_____

_____

<A model answer is provided in the Answer key on page 110.>

# 20 Revision 2

## Practice exercises

1   Write an appropriate word in each blank space of the Writing Task 1 introduction based on the figure below. Then complete the report in your own words.

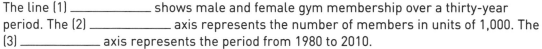

The line (1) _____ shows male and female gym membership over a thirty-year period. The (2) _____ axis represents the number of members in units of 1,000. The (3) _____ axis represents the period from 1980 to 2010.

⟨ A model answer is provided in the Answer key on page 110. ⟩

**2**  Read the passage below and underline words and expressions which are similar in meaning to expressions 1–6 in the box.

**1**  deterioration     **3**  changed gradually     **5**  barely changed

**2**  giving up         **4**  forty years          **6**  about thirty years ago

The aim of this study was to critically assess the popular belief that a decline in the quality of parenting is largely responsible for the reported rise in anti-social behaviour among young people. The study was undertaken in response to numerous articles in the popular press and elsewhere criticizing parents for abandoning traditional child–rearing practices. The authors' findings suggest that parenting styles have indeed evolved over the past four decades, though not in the way one might expect. According to the researchers, parents today monitor their children much more intensively than they did a generation ago; moreover, parental expectations of good behaviour have also steadily increased. The incidence of conduct problems, on the other hand, appears to have hardly altered. The authors conclude that the quality of parenting, if anything, seems to have improved, and that conduct problems would be significantly more acute if parents had not developed greater responsiveness to the needs of their children.

**3**  Underline the word in italics that fits correctly into each sentence 1–7 below.

**1**  In academic writing, it is important to *differ/distinguish* between fact and opinion.

**2**  These two £50 notes look *resemble/identical*, but one of them is a fake.

**3**  In terms of energy consumed, running two kilometres is *alike/equivalent* to swimming twenty lengths in a swimming pool.

**4**  The quality of student accommodation here *varies/differentiates*, but the price is more or less the same.

**5**  All mothers are women; *conversely/contrary*, not all women are mothers.

**6**  The university is recruiting more international students in order to create a more *distinct/diverse* student body.

**7**  The two dancers were *comparable/compare* in terms of technique, but the younger one was much more expressive.

**4**  Listen to sentences 1–7 and indicate whether the expressions below are causes or consequences.

**1**  reduced government expenditure

**2**  drilling for oil under the sea

**3**  more women in 'men's' jobs

**4**  lack of employment opportunities

**5**  success in life

**6**  alarm in farming communities

**7**  too much cleaning

**5** Combine each pair of sentences 1–6 below using the word or expression in brackets. Make any other necessary changes.

**1** She knew she did not have the right qualifications. She applied for the job. (*nevertheless*)

**2** Geography is the study of the countries of the world. Geology is the study of the structure and origin of the earth. (*whereas*)

**3** Over the last ten years, there has been a marked divergence in the salaries of executives and the salaries of ordinary workers. Executive pay has increased by one hundred and eighty–seven per cent, while average pay has increased by only twenty-seven per cent. (*the former/the latter*)

**4** Shopkeepers should be penalized if they sell cigarettes to young people. The minimum age at which young people can legally buy tobacco products should be increased to eighteen. (*moreover*)

**5** In many countries, it is very difficult to train for a new career after the age of forty. People need to think carefully before choosing an occupation. (*hence*)

**6** There was a dispute over land ownership. The two communities had lived harmoniously for many years. (*prior*)

**6** Listen to speakers 1–7 and indicate whether the statements below are True or False.

**1** Speaker one is sure her uncle will retire at 65.

**2** Speaker two completely agrees that nurses should be paid more.

**3** Speaker three's employers have decided to give her time off to study.

**4** Speaker four suspects that Jim did not write the essay himself.

**5** Speaker five doesn't mind renting a flat.

**6** Speaker six believes that there will be more traffic because of the new supermarket.

**7** Speaker seven isn't sure that she'd like to stay in Japan.

**7** Listen to this Speaking Part 2 based on the following task:

> Describe a problem you have experienced during your work or studies.
>
> You should say:
>
> > how the problem arose
> >
> > what you did in response
> >
> > what the outcome was
>
> and explain what you learned from the experience.

**When you are ready, try the task yourself. You can make some notes to help you if you wish.**

🎧 8   **Listen to speakers 1–6 and complete the sentences below by writing one word in each gap:**

38

1   There is little evidence to support the _____ that men and women communicate differently.

2   Conspiracy theories explaining the company takeover lack _____.

3   The argument in support of developing a new widget is a _____ one.

4   The case against the chief executive is founded on _____ not facts.

5   The arguments in favour of independence are _____.

6   The minister's position on deregulation is _____.

9   **For each sentence 1–6 choose which sentence, a or b, is the most similar in meaning.**

1   There is ample evidence that regular exercise can reduce the severity of depression.

   a   Regular exercise has been proven to reduce the severity of depression.

   b   There is good reason for believing that regular exercise can reduce the severity of depression.

2   The army crossed the border, ostensibly in pursuit of rebels.

   a   The army said that they were pursuing rebels, but this was probably not the real reason they crossed the border.

   b   The army crossed the border, probably because they were pursuing rebels.

3   The cost of living is marginally higher than it was at the same time last year.

   a   Most things are bit more expensive now than they were this time last year.

   b   Most things are a lot more expensive now than they were this time last year.

4   The trade dispute between the two countries has reportedly been resolved.

   a   People say the two countries' trade dispute has been resolved.

   b   We can be sure the two countries' trade dispute has been resolved.

5   The bicycle tyres were recalled by the manufacturer because they were liable to burst in certain circumstances.

   a   The manufacturer recalled the bicycle tyres because they had burst in certain circumstances.

   b   The manufacturer recalled the bicycle tyres because they could burst in certain circumstances.

6   Grandfather's wish to live in his own home is undisputed; we're just not sure whether he can actually manage it.

   a   We doubt whether grandfather really can or wants to live at home.

   b   We know grandfather wants to live at home but we doubt whether he can.

# Audio script

## Unit 1  People and relationships

### Track 01

**1**  I've learned a lot from so many people, but I suppose the person that stands out is my colleague Lin. When I started working at the firm, my employer didn't give me a lot of formal training so I had to learn on the job. I was given the desk next to Lin and she explained everything to me. She was incredibly efficient. She knew the job so well, and she made it look so easy.

**2**  The person I admire the most is probably my boss. She really knows what she wants to achieve with the organization, but at the same time she is so flexible and open to new ideas. She really takes an interest not only in her clients but also in her employees. She really listens to what they have to say.

**3**  I suppose the relationship I've found most difficult – but ultimately most rewarding – has been my relationship with my younger brother. He's different from me in almost every way you can imagine. I'm the kind of person who likes to get things done, but he is a real dreamer – so idealistic. It used to drive me crazy, but over the years, I've come to really admire him for following his dreams.

### Track 02

I'm going to begin this section of my talk by saying something about only children, that is children without siblings. Historically, only children were relatively uncommon. However, these days, as families are becoming smaller, being an only child has become relatively more common. There are many reasons for this trend – social, economic, and political, which I won't go into at this point. However, I will say that having an only child generally means that parental resources can be concentrated on the one child. And I would add that, by parental resources I mean not just money but also care and attention.

Only children have frequently been seen as different from children with siblings and subjected to negative stereotype. They are often considered to be less tolerant of others – i.e. less able to accept differences, to allow those with different points of view to say and do as they like. Not surprisingly, they are sometimes said to be less co-operative than other children – in other words, less able to work effectively with others. On the other hand, only children are often highly regarded for their autonomy, that is to say, their ability to make their own decisions without being unduly influenced by others. In short, the picture that's emerging is of children who are rather unconventional, that is not quite 'normal' in social terms.

I think it's important to say here that many of these views have been challenged. In fact more recent research has found that only children are in fact very similar to children with siblings...

## Track 03

The subject of my talk today is the relationship between birth order and personality. By birth order I mean whether an individual is the firstborn child in the family, a middle child, an only child, and so on.

The belief that birth order has a lasting impact on personality is widespread and frequently referred to in popular psychology literature. Alfred Adler, an Austrian psychotherapist, was one of the first to suggest that there was a connection between birth order and personality. He noticed that firstborn children experienced a loss of status with the birth of siblings. According to Adler, this made eldest children more likely to be anxious than other children. However, on the positive side, they also tend to be conscientious and achievement-oriented, perhaps because they want to regain a position of primacy within the family.

Since Adler, there have been many attempts to establish links between birth order and a range of personality traits. Some studies have found that last-born children tend to be more extrovert and agreeable, that is, they not only seek out the company of others but also tend to get along well with other people. Middle children, on the other hand, are more likely to be rebellious, perhaps in an attempt to define themselves as 'special' in relation to their more conscientious elder siblings and agreeable younger siblings. Some studies, for example, have found that middle children are more likely to choose unconventional careers and hobbies.

However, whilst these views are widely held among the public, scholars have more recently cast doubt on their validity. Many studies have been found to employ a flawed methodology, for instance failing to adequately consider variables such as the family's socio-economic status. Large-scale meta-analyses of studies have proved inconclusive with no single trait consistently associated with a given position within the family. Nevertheless, most people are intuitively drawn to the idea that birth order has an effect on the sort of people we become.

# Unit 4   Adventure

**Speaker 1:** We had booked an excursion to the beach but chose to venture into the hills instead, hoping to see some of the local wildlife.

**Speaker 2:** Many young people in their twenties seek adventure; that's why they come to places like Thailand and Jamaica.

**Speaker 3:** We looked all over the town and eventually found a local guide to accompany us to the nearest village.

**Speaker 4:** We won't be back until the end of August. Because of the disturbances, we had to reschedule our journey for the following week.

**Speaker 5:** I think you'll find your trip down the Amazon quite an adventure. You can expect to encounter some pretty strange insects in the rainforest.

**Speaker 6:** While backpacking around Thailand, I had to learn to overcome difficulties by myself. I can't count the number of times I got lost!

## Track 05

I had the most amazing adventure last year. I spent an afternoon exploring the caves near my village with a group of friends. None of us had ever been caving before, so we went with my friend's brother, who's been doing it for ages. He supplied all the equipment and showed us what to do and how to stay safe.

The route down into the earth was really narrow in places. It was quite an intense experience. At one point, I was completely wedged in between two sheets of rock. It was a struggle to stay calm. Eventually I was able to work my way free and continue the journey.

After what seemed like ages the tunnel opened up into this huge space underground. It was damp and pitch black – full of echoes and other strange noises. I could hear something flapping but I couldn't see what it was. We had to tread carefully and hang onto each other as the ground was very uneven and there were pools of water all over the place, goodness knows how deep. We slowly worked our way around and back out the way we came in.

I suppose I chose to go on this adventure because I needed a challenge. I tend to get nervous in small spaces, so this was an opportunity to try to overcome my fears. Also, this was the last summer we were going to be together before heading off to university, so it was good to do something special, something memorable.

I felt really proud of myself at the end of it. It was a valuable experience. I learned that it's really liberating to face your fears. It also confirmed something that I suppose I've always known: friendship is priceless! There's no way I could have done it on my own.

# Unit 5   Gadgets

## Track 06

The pinhole camera is a very simple device. It consists of a cylinder with a radius of approximately 4 cm and a height of 12 cm. There is a small hole 1 mm in diameter positioned halfway up the wall of the cylinder. A sheet of photographic paper 18 cm in width curves round the inside of the cylinder leaving a gap of about 1 cm just behind the pinhole. The camera is very simple to use, but it takes a long time to produce a picture. If you fix the camera outside and expose it to the light, after a few minutes, you will find that an image has appeared on the photographic paper.

## Track 07

1   You may need to adjust the volume of the microphone so that we can hear you at the back of the room.

2   If we launch the game in January, we're unlikely to maximize sales.

3   These types of comments reinforce the notion that the unemployed don't want to work.

4   After lengthy negotiations, the contractor was able to secure a good deal.

5   The organization has suspended operations until more money becomes available.

## Track 08

**Lisa:**   OK, as I understand it, we've got to build a device that will allow us to convey a ping-pong ball from one table to another a metre away. Bill, what have we got?

**Bill:**   We're only allowed to use: six sheets of paper, a box of paper clips, some thread, four drinking straws, and two elastic bands.

**Lisa:**   I'm not sure where to start. Anybody got any ideas?

**Omar:**   Maybe we could use the elastic bands to launch the ball across the gap...

**Bill:**   That's not a bad idea, Omar, but I think that would be rather difficult to do. Hmmm...I think we should create a sort of bridge with the sheets of paper. We could suspend it between the tables.

**Omar:**   How would that work?

**Bill:**   We could cut the paper into strips of about 10 cm wide...

**Lisa:**   I get it!...and attach them end-to-end with paper clips. But how would we secure the bridge to the table?

**Omar:**   We could use thread for that – I'm sure we could work something out. But what I'm not sure about is how we can keep the ball from falling off the bridge.

| Lisa: | Well, if we fold the sides of the paper so that it forms a cylinder or tube that would keep the ball from rolling onto the floor. This would also help keep the bridge rigid enough to span the distance between the tables. What do you think Bill? |
|---|---|
| Bill: | I think that's a brilliant idea. If necessary we could use the drinking straws to further reinforce the structure. |
| Omar: | Do you think 10 cm strips would be wide enough? What's the diameter of a ping-pong ball? |
| Lisa: | That's a good question Omar. I don't know maybe two and a half centimetres – OK what about 15 cm? |

# Unit 8   Getting involved

## Track 09

**1**

| | |
|---|---|
| **Reader:** | The Owl and the Pussy-cat went to sea<br>In a beautiful pea-green boat,<br>They took some honey, and plenty of money,<br>Wrapped up in a five-pound note... |

**2**

| | |
|---|---|
| **Presenter:** | Now I wonder, Minister, whether you'd like to say something about the government's proposals for banking reform. |
| **Minister:** | Yes, thank-you. As I think we all recognize, the need for change in the banking sector is long overdue. |

**3**

| | |
|---|---|
| **Commentator:** | Michalski plays it into the penalty area ... to Dembinski. Dembinski out to Bajor. ... Bajor beats one man, crosses the ball into the centre ... |

**4**

| | |
|---|---|
| **Presenter:** | And now we'll hear Dvořák's Symphony Number 9 in E Minor 'From the New World', Opus 95, popularly known as the New World Symphony. |

**5**

| | |
|---|---|
| **Man:** | But darling, I said nothing of the sort! |
| **Woman:** | You most certainly did! Peter was there! He saw everything... |
| **Man:** | Surely you're not going to take Peter's word for it... |

## Track 10

| | |
|---|---|
| **Speaker 1:** | In my second year I helped set up the university radio station. It used to broadcast everything from campus news to local bands. |
| **Speaker 2:** | As a secondary school pupil I participated in regional and national debates around the country. It was challenging, and very rewarding. |
| **Speaker 3:** | I've enjoyed concerts ever since I was a child. I used to love watching the conductor – I wanted to be one myself for a time. |
| **Speaker 4:** | I was editor of the student magazine for a while. People sent in all kinds of articles. I had to choose what to include and then put it all together. |
| **Speaker 5:** | I used to attend gallery openings all the time. I love contemporary art. Haven't got much time for it now, unfortunately, |

## Track 11

| | | | | |
|---|---|---|---|---|
| **1** affairs | **2** assemble | **3** broadcast | **4** classical | **5** establish |
| **6** observe | **7** orchestra | **8** advise | **9** resign | |

## Track 12

**Examiner:** What do you enjoy doing when you're not working or studying?

**Candidate:** Well, ...I've been involved in amateur dramatics for quite a while now. I started out as an actor, taking small parts, but now I'm directing a play. It's a comedy about university life – written by the students.

**Examiner:** Tell me more about what that involves.

**Candidate:** Basically, I'm responsible for directing what happens on stage. I have to tell the actors what to do. I have to make sure the sets are all right – and the lighting, things like that.

**Examiner:** How did you first get started?

**Candidate:** I wasn't interested in theatre at all, or acting – I was quite a shy person. But my room-mate had a small part in a play and I used to go along to their rehearsals. One day he was ill and I stood in for him. I loved it.

**Examiner:** What else do you enjoy doing in your spare time?

**Candidate:** Er ... I quite like listening to music. When I'm free in the evening, I like to go out and see local bands. I'm hoping that someday I'll see a band that becomes really famous.

## Track 13

What do you enjoy doing when you're not working or studying?
Tell me more about what that involves.
How did you first get started?
What else do you enjoy doing in your spare time?

# Unit 9    Global warming

## Track 14

Hurricanes have heavy rains and are therefore more likely to cause floods. Droughts occur when there is a lack of rainfall.

Hurricanes and typhoons are both violent storms that develop over water. If the storm develops in the Atlantic or Caribbean it is referred to as a hurricane. If it develops in the Pacific, it is known as a typhoon.

The largest glaciers in the world are found in the polar ice caps of Antarctica and Greenland. Glaciers are also found in mountains.

A current is a steady flowing movement of air or water.

## Track 15

1 **Sentence a:**    In freezing temperatures, water turns into ice and expands.

  **Sentence b:**    Metal, on the other hand, contracts when cold.

2 **Sentence a:**    It is highly likely that glaciers will continue to melt.

  **Sentence b:**    It is unlikely that they will melt as quickly as some climate experts had predicted.

3 **Sentence a:**    Previous predictions were based on inaccurate data.

  **Sentence b:**    More accurate information is now available.

4 **Sentence a:**    Some climate scientists may have overestimated the rate of global warming.

  **Sentence b:**    Others may have underestimated the impact of climate change.

## Track 16

In today's talk I'm going to give you an overview of the most recent thinking on climate change. Recently the IGPCC – the Intergovernmental Panel on Climate Change – has conducted a major review of the evidence for climate change. In its conclusions, it states that the evidence for global warming continues to be overwhelming. However, according to the panel, some of the risk factors identified in earlier reports have been overstated, whereas other impacts of global warming may have been understated. In this talk, I'm going to outline some of the overstated risk factors and explain the current position on each. I'll then mention briefly some of the aspects of global warming that are now considered to be a more serious problem than previously thought.

One of the most significant revisions in the new report concerns estimates of rising sea levels. Previous studies had predicted that sea levels would rise by more than two metres. The latest evidence suggests that sea levels are likely to rise by no more than one metre. This is good news for many coastal areas as flood defences currently in place are much more likely to cope with a rise of one metre. A rise of two metres would have required major investment in flood defences.

The reason climate scientists have come up with such different predictions of sea level rises has to do with our understanding of what is happening to the major glaciers and ice sheets around the world. Some appear to be contracting faster than predicted, and others appear to be expanding. In 2007, for example, the IGPCC predicted that the Arctic would be ice free in summer by 2080. The latest predictions bring this date forward by 20 years to 2060. In the Antarctic, on the other hand, the ice sheet appears to be expanding as sea water freezes over. This variability in ice sheet activity accounts for the differences in our predictions of rising sea levels.

Another significant revision of our understanding of climate change concerns the Gulf Stream. As many of you probably know, the Gulf Stream is a current of warm sea water that travels from the tropics northeastwards across the Atlantic. It is responsible for keeping temperatures in Europe and North America 5–10 degrees warmer than they would be otherwise. An earlier study concluded that the flow rate of the Gulf Stream had decreased by 30 per cent since the 1950s. It warned that the northern hemisphere could be heading for another ice age, in other words, a period of prolonged cold. However, a more recent study has indicated that currents of warm water have actually accelerated in the last 20 years. Climate scientists now believe that these differences are due to natural variability and that the Gulf Stream is unlikely to disappear. This is good news for those who live in Europe and North America.

I'd like to move on now and mention some of the consequences of global warming and some of the risk factors which may have been underestimated by previous studies. As far as consequences go, there is new evidence that tropical forests are more susceptible to drought than previously thought and that the severity of severe weather events such as hurricanes and typhoons may have been underestimated in the past. This is particularly bad news for those who live in southern regions. More worrying, there is stronger evidence that thawing permafrost in northern regions is producing very high emissions of methane gas. As I explained in an earlier lecture, methane is a much more potent greenhouse gas than carbon dioxide. This thawing ground has the potential to significantly exacerbate climate change. I therefore have to conclude this talk by saying that, in spite of the good news on rising sea levels, global warming continues to be a serious cause for concern. To ignore it would be most irresponsible.

# Unit 10 Revision 1

## Track 17

1 It's definitely a bacterium and not a virus that's caused your inflammation, so I'm going to prescribe a course of antibiotics.

2 I suggest that over the next six months you follow a reduced-calorie diet and exercise for 30 minutes three times a week. Come and see me in four weeks' time and we'll see how you're getting on.

3 You appear to have developed a sensitivity to pollen. You may need to stay indoors at certain times of the year and take antihistamines to improve your condition.

4 I think your headaches may be due to the fact that you haven't been taking in enough fluids. You really need to drink at least a litre of water a day.

5 I'm afraid you're going to continue to experience some weakness in your left-hand side. I've referred you to the physiotherapist and prescribed medication to prevent a further occurrence.

## Track 18

1 It took us forever to get out of the city. We must have driven for an hour and a half – nothing but shopping malls and bungalows as far as the eye could see.

2 I don't mind the grime, the crime or the noise. And the skyscrapers are just amazing. It's a vertical city. You really need to see it to believe it.

3 We stayed in a lovely little cottage, surrounded by meadows. It was gorgeous – so peaceful.

4 The High Street is thronged during the festival. Street performers, clowns, acrobats, all kinds of people peddling all kinds of crazy things. You'd love it.

5 I'd read so much about it when I was at school. I couldn't believe I was actually there, an ancient town, almost perfectly preserved. You weren't allowed to take photographs, but I did anyway – when no-one was looking, of course.

## Track 19

1 I was never cut out to be an engineer. I just can't do the maths. So, yes, on the whole I think changing over to product design was the right decision for me.

2 Whenever we got together to revise, she'd end up moaning about her landlord. She was a good student, but looking back I don't think the arrangement really worked.

3 I can understand why universities may want to increase tuition fees, but if they increase them threefold, only the rich will be able to afford it.

4 I see the pass rates have gone up again this year. That would never have happened in my day, even though we were much better informed than kids nowadays.

5 Basically, it allows me to pursue my interest in music and keep my job in the recording studio. It's not so intense either. I've got time to think about what I'm learning, absorb it at my own pace.

# Unit 12   Words for describing change

**1  Examiner:**   How are schools today different from schools in your parents' generation?

   **Candidate:**   There is much less discipline and pupils are difficult to control. Standards of behaviour have really declined.

**2  Examiner:**   In what ways has the countryside in your country changed during your lifetime?

   **Candidate:**   There are far fewer young people living in the countryside. Many of them have had to abandon rural life and move to the cities to look for work.

**3  Examiner:**   What do you think is the most significant change in the way people communicate?

   **Candidate:**   Social networking sites – definitely. Just look at the way they've evolved over the last few years. You could almost spark a revolution with a click of a mouse.

**4  Examiner:**   What do you think will be the most significant change in people's life style in the next ten or twenty years?

   **Candidate:**   I think as energy becomes more expensive, we will have to modify how we live – consume less, conserve more.

**5  Examiner:**   In what ways has the experience of living abroad affected you?

   **Candidate:**   I've had to learn to adjust to different ways of doing things – shopping, cooking, socializing – all sorts of things.

**6  Examiner:**   How, in your view, are patterns of employment in your country likely to change in the next few years?

   **Candidate:**   Many more people are going to work in financial services. That whole sector is developing very rapidly in my country. There are lots of opportunities now.

## Track 21

1  I grew up in a village that looks much as it did five centuries ago. Almost nothing has altered.

2  Job security has diminished over the last few years. It's almost impossible to find long-term work let alone a job for life.

3  I think over the next decade, surgical techniques will become increasingly refined. Surgeons will be able to perform operations that we can only dream of now.

4  Within a generation, attitudes towards authority have shifted. Nowadays, people are more likely to challenge authority figures.

5  Unless we transform the way we live, we're unlikely to survive into the next millennium.

## Track 22
**1** abandon **2** adjust **3** alter **4** decline **5** develop **6** diminish
**7** evolve **8** modify **9** refine **10** shift **11** transform **12** century
**13** decade **14** generation **15** millennium

## Track 23

**1** Do you think people are more adventurous now than in the past?

**2** Why, in your view, have attitudes towards risk changed?

**3** What sort of adventures do you think people will be having in ten or twenty years' time?

## Track 24
**Examiner:** Do you think people are more adventurous now than in the past?

**Candidate:** On the whole, yes, I think they are. When I compare young people today with my parent's generation, I would say that attitudes have shifted. People expect more from life and want to develop personally as well as professionally. People are looking for experiences that will transform them in some way – give them new insights. For example, many people my age want to travel abroad and experience very different life styles.

**Examiner:** Why, in your view, have attitudes towards risk changed?

**Candidate:** I suppose society has evolved. There is a greater emphasis on independence and originality. You can't develop these qualities without taking risks. In my country, previous generations were more likely to conform. People would adjust their behaviour so as not to stand out too much. These days, people want to be a bit different; they want to stand out from the crowd.

**Examiner:** What sort of adventures do you think people will be having in ten or twenty years' time?

**Candidate:** I think as tourism extends into every corner of the world, interest in foreign travel as a form of adventure will diminish. People will look for adventure closer to home, maybe by being more creative – doing things that haven't been done before. I have a friend who's lost his job and had to abandon his plans to travel abroad. He's going to see how far he can get by travelling on local buses. I think he's calculated that he can get halfway across the country. It will be quite an adventure!

# Unit 13   Words expressing similarity and difference

## Track 25

1   Victor and Vincent are identical twins.

2   Boys and girls rarely think alike.

3   We enjoy watching a diverse range of films.

4   Psychiatry and psychology are two distinct disciplines.

5   The average cost of a house today is equivalent to six years' average annual salary.

6   The minister was sacked for expressing views that were contrary to those of the government.

7   The majority of female respondents reported spending more on sugary snacks; conversely, the majority of male respondents said they had spent more on savoury snacks.

8   People who do similar work should receive comparable rates of pay.

## Track 26

1   In order to stay healthy it is important to eat a varied diet.

2   The risk of flying in a light aircraft is comparable to that of sailing in a small boat.

3   He decided to accept my recommendation, which was based on a detailed comparison of the two courses.

4   There is a remarkable resemblance between this song and one that was recorded thirty years ago.

5   Every student in the class interpreted the essay question differently.

6   The opinions he expresses in his blog are often in complete contrast to those he expresses on television.

7   The lecturer contrasted the last three major economic crises.

## Track 27

Many people today complain of job-related stress. Indeed numerous surveys have shown that most working adults today perceive the workplace to be a more challenging environment than in previous generations.

Although on the surface of it, stressful work and challenging work may appear to be identical, it is important to distinguish between the two terms. Job stress occurs when the demands of a job do not match the worker's needs, resources or skills. A teacher who is required to teach a subject he or she knows nothing about or is not interested in is likely to experience job stress. Prolonged job stress can result in poor physical or emotional health, or what we call 'burnout'.

A challenging job is very different in that it encourages the worker to develop skills and resources. Meeting a challenge is rewarding. It is comparable to stretching out to grasp a prize that is nearly within reach. Challenging work can be energizing and contribute to a greater sense of well-being. In fact an appropriate level of challenge is essential for good physical and emotional health.

While we often see some jobs as being inherently stressful or challenging, it is important to remember that these qualities are a function of the match between the worker and the job. Two workers may well have very different experiences of the same job as no two workers are alike. What is a stressful job for one may well be a challenging job for another.

# Unit 16   Adverbs

## Track 28

1   Surprisingly, the prime minister has been elected for a second term.

2   Interestingly, more young people voted in this election than in the previous one.

3   Absolutely! I'd love to return to Africa some day.

4   Supposedly, travel broadens the mind.

5   Undoubtedly, cooking with natural ingredients is better for your health.

6   Inevitably, the cost of fuel will rise.

7   Presumably, fewer people will travel by car if petrol becomes too expensive.

## Track 29

**1** absolutely   **2** necessarily   **3** particularly   **4** presumably   **5** supposedly   **6** surprisingly

## Track 30

Tell me about the house or flat you live in.
How do you feel about living there?
Is the decoration or appearance of the place you live important to you?
When choosing things for your flat, is the appearance of an object more important to you than how well it works?

## Track 31

Hello. My name is Susan Davie. Can you tell me your full name, please?

Thanks. Can I please see your identification?... Thanks, that's great. I'm going to ask you some questions about yourself now.

Tell me about your favourite film or television programme.
How do you think television has changed since you were a child?
Are there any types of programmes that you don't like to watch?

I'd like to ask you a few questions about transport. How do you normally travel to your work or place of study?
How do people in your country normally travel?
How easy is it to get around in your country?

We're now going to talk about places of interest in your country. What do you think is the most interesting building or monument in your country?
Do you prefer historic building styles to modern architecture?
To what extent do people in your country value traditional architecture?

# Unit 17   Words for problems and solutions

## Track 32

1   As I was getting into the car I saw the crack in the windscreen. I have no idea how it happened, but it's going to be expensive to repair.

2   My grandmother's feeling poorly and lost her appetite. I'm afraid she's not as strong as she used to be, but I don't know what I can do to help.

3   I've just been told that I've got to show my identification card to get a new key for my locker. But I think I left my ID in the locker before I lost my key. What a ridiculous situation!

4   I think you'd better come home straight away. That big tree in the garden has come down onto the power line in front of the house. It looks really dangerous.

5   I've just been invited to go to Alaska with my brother and his wife – it's the trip of a lifetime! But I should really save the money to pay for my course. I just can't decide what to do.

## Track 33

1   Don't worry. The damage to your car can be easily repaired.

2   I'm sure you'd like to do more to alleviate her suffering.

3   If you speak to the manager, she may be able to resolve your predicament.

4   I'll be right over! That's not a crisis you should tackle on your own.

5   You're never going to resolve that dilemma until you decide what you really want.

## Track 34

Good morning everyone. I'm Kerry Wilson, one of the student welfare team, and I'm going to talk to you about how to deal with some of the difficulties that may arise while you're studying with us. Of course we hope that you won't experience any problems during your studies, but it's good to know what help is available should anything go wrong.

I know some of you have had a problem opening a bank account and that you are anxious about paying your course fees. If you're in this predicament, don't worry. To open an account you need to present evidence that you are enrolled on a full-time course. Just go to the Language Centre office and ask for a letter of enrolment. As long as you have registered for the course, you can get a letter. You don't need to have paid your fees.

For those of you who are living in private accommodation, we would advise you to speak to one of the student welfare team before signing a lease. Sometimes disputes can arise, for example in relation to damage to property. If you have a disagreement with your landlord, one of the welfare team can intervene if necessary.

Finally, the student welfare office can be phoned at any time during the day or night in case of an emergency. If your room is burgled for example, do not hesitate to phone the emergency number in your welfare handbook. This type of crisis is very rare, but please be assured that help is available should you require it.

# Unit 20   Revision 2

### Track 35

1  Government cuts to public spending triggered a second economic downturn.

2  Many environmentalists believe that the offshore oil industry has resulted in significant damage to marine life.

3  Interestingly, the Second World War contributed to the expansion of female employment, in particular, the increase in numbers of women doing jobs typically reserved for men.

4  A number of commentators have said that the recent public disorder stems from the high rates of youth unemployment.

5  Some people even believe that your genes determine whether or not you succeed in life.

6  The return of wolves to southern regions of Europe has provoked fear and anger among many farmers.

7  There is evidence that some skin conditions can result from excessive cleanliness.

### Track 36

**Speaker 1:**   My uncle turns 65 next year, at which point he'll presumably retire.

**Speaker 2:**   Do I think nurses should be better paid? Absolutely!

**Speaker 3:**   My employers have provisionally agreed to give me time off to complete my studies.

**Speaker 4:**   Supposedly, Jim wrote the essay himself, but it looks to me like he had a bit of help.

**Speaker 5:**   Ideally, I'd like to buy a flat of my own, but unfortunately, it looks like I'll have to rent for a few more years.

**Speaker 6:**   Inevitably, the new supermarket is going to bring more cars into the area.

**Speaker 7:**   I'd like to stay in Japan indefinitely, but I'm not sure that's going to be possible.

## Track 37

I guess one of the most difficult dilemmas I've faced concerns a colleague Lydia, who also happens to be a friend. I'd been given the task of organizing a series of social events for a group of schoolchildren visiting from Germany and I thought it would be a great idea to work with Lydia, so I persuaded my boss to assign her to me as an assistant. I have to say, it was a mistake from the start. Lydia was so disorganized, kept forgetting what she was to do, lost track of what she'd paid for and so on. I suppose, looking back she just didn't have the experience or the skills for the job. Don't get me wrong, she was a great laugh and we're still friends, but I had to work overtime to sort everything out. Looking back I can see that I didn't really address the problem directly. I just covered up for her mistakes and made sure the programme ran smoothly. I didn't want my boss to intervene. I suppose I felt partly to blame because I hadn't really thought carefully about whether she was really suitable for the job. Anyway, that experience has taught me that it's safer to keep friendship and work matters separate.

## Track 38

1   I don't really subscribe to the notion that men and women have fundamentally different styles of communication. Where's the evidence?

2   You really have to question the credibility of some of the conspiracy theories surrounding the assassination.

3   I didn't think we should invest in developing a new widget, but he put forward a valid argument and I'm now prepared to go along with it.

4   The accusation that the chief executive knew about the illegal activities of his employees is based on pure conjecture.

5   The case for independence is now so compelling I can't see an alternative course of action.

6   The minister's stance of deregulation is bound to be biased – he's got a considerable financial interest in the industry.

# Answer key

## 1 People and relationships

### Practice exercises

**1** Circle: parent, sibling, spouse
Underline: client, colleague, employer

**2** 1 d  2 f  3 c

**3** 1 efficient  2 flexible  4 idealistic

**4** 1 c  2 d  3 a  4 b  5 e  6 c

**5** 1 siblings  2 care, attention  3 differences
4 effectively, others  5 make, decisions  6 normal

### Exam practice

1 C  2 B  3 A  4 C  5 B

## 2 Health

### Practice exercises

**1** Circle: heart disease, allergies,
obesity, stroke, addiction
Underline: infection, dehydration
**3** 1 health conditions, diseases  2 addiction
3 infectious agents  4 immunizing
**4** 1 admit  2 examine  3 diagnose  4 treat
5 discharge
**5** 1 e  2 c  3 b  4 a  5 d

### Exam practice

1 True  2 Not given  3 True  4 True  5 burden
6 is diagnosed  7 who took part

## 3 Education

### Practice exercises

**1** 1 archaeology – b
2 astronomy – g
3 economics – d
4 geology – e
5 linguistics – f
6 psychology – a
7 sociology – c
**2** 1 astronomer  2 psychology  3 Linguistics
4 economists  5 geology  6 sociology
7 archaeologists

**3**

| verb | noun | adjective |
| --- | --- | --- |
| claim | claim | × |
| define | definition | × |
| evaluate | evaluation | evaluative |
| investigate | investigation | investigative |
| X | evidence | evident |
| hypothesize | hypothesis | hypothetical |
| theorize | theory | theoretical |

**4** 1 define  2 evaluative  3 investigate
4 evident  5 hypothesis  6 theoretical
**5** 1 evaluate  2 hypothesis  3 evidence
4 investigation  5 definition

### Exam practice

1 claim  2 evaluate  3 define  4 Linguists
5 analyses  6 Archaeologists  7 investigate
8 geology  9 astronomers  10 evidence

## 4 Adventure

### Practice exercises

**1** 1 c  2 f  3 a  4 b  5 d  6 e
<u>ven</u>ture  <u>seek</u>  ac<u>com</u>pany  re<u>sch</u>edule
en<u>coun</u>ter  over<u>come</u>

**2**  1 a look for          5 a journey
1 b seek            5 b itinerary
2 a dreary          6 a profound
2 b dull            6 b intense
3 a destination     7 a significant
3 b goal            7 b pivotal
4 a encounter       8 a valuable
4 b meet            8 b priceless

**3** 1 itinerary  2 seek  3 journey  4 encounter
5 dreary  6 pivotal  7 meet  8 profound

### Exam practice

1 exploring  2 intense  3 journey  4 challenge
5 overcome  6 valuable  7 priceless

# 5   Gadgets

## Practice exercises

**1** 1 d   2 b   3 g   4 c   5 a   6 f   7 h   8 e
**2** 1 4 cm   2 12 cm   3 1 mm   4 18 cm
**3** 1 suspend   2 reinforce   3 adjust
   4 launch   5 secure
**4** 1 a   2 b   3 b   4 a   5 a

## Exam practice

1 C   2 B   3 A   4 C   5 A   6 B

# 6   Cities

## Practice exercises

**1** 1 bustling   2 busy   3 pioneering
   4 extensive   5 historic
**2** 1 public transport   2 housing   3 amenity
   4 infrastructure
**3** a 1   b 1   c 2   d 2   e 3   f 1   g 1   h 2
**4** 3

## Exam practice

1 iv   2 iii   3 vi   4 vii

# 7   The art of persuasion

## Practice exercises

**1** 1 d   2 b   3 a   4 c
**2** 1 advocate   2 acknowledge   3 justified
   4 outline   5 object (to)
**3** 1 b   2 e   3 a   4 c   5 d
**4** 1 Consumers question whether the new printer
   will be more reliable than previous models.
   2 Many people object to the sale of national
   treasures abroad.
   3 Most people acknowledge that the National
   Health Service has improved the nation's health.
   4 Some politicians assert that new approaches
   to tackling youth crime should be explored.
   5 Experts dispute these figures.
   6 The teacher implied that Susan
   would pass the course.

## Exam practice model answer

There has been considerable debate in recent years over the role of free speech in a free society. Some object to absolute freedom of speech. Others advocate free speech, arguing that the ability to tolerate different points of view is a hallmark of civilized society. Whilst I acknowledge that there are strong arguments on both sides, I would suggest that freedom of speech should be protected in all but extreme circumstances. In this essay, I will outline two main reasons.

Firstly, if people are not allowed to express their views freely, they may choose to take action instead. This is how the communist regimes of Eastern Europe were toppled in the 1980s. The same is happening again in other regions of the world today. People may choose to behave destructively, to riot, for example, when they have no other means of being heard.

Secondly, history shows that great thinkers of the past have often been censored for ideas that are now widely accepted as valid. The sixteenth-century astronomer Galileo, for example, was condemned for advocating a sun-centered theory of the solar system. More recently, many dissident writers, scientists and thinkers who had been silenced in the former Soviet Bloc have come to be celebrated for their achievements.

In short, freedom of speech is essential for a peaceful, just and progressive society. It may be challenging for society to allow differences of opinion out into the open; however, the consequences of restricting free speech are likely to be more damaging in the longer term.
(*253 words*)

# 8   Getting involved

## Practice exercises

**1** 1 d   2 a   3 b   4 c   5 e
**2**

|            | interest | involvement |
|------------|----------|-------------|
| Speaker 1  | e        | iii         |
| Speaker 2  | c        | ii          |
| Speaker 3  | d        | i           |
| Speaker 4  | a        | iii         |
| Speaker 5  | b        | i           |

**3** a iv   b v   c i   d iii   e ii
**4** 1 ii   2 c   3 v   4 iii   5 a
**5** 1 /z/   2 /s/   3 /s/   4 /s/   5 /s/   6 /z/   7 /s/
   8 /z/   9 /z/

# 9   Global warming

## Practice exercises

**1** 1 glaciers   2 typhoons   3 droughts
   4 current   5 flood   6 hurricane
**2** 1 a flood
   2 hurricanes originate in the Caribbean or Atlantic;
   typhoons originate in the Pacific
   3 polar icecaps of Antarctica and Greenland, and in
   mountains
   4 both air and water

**3** 1 disagree   2 inconsistent   3 unlikely
   4 illegal   5 irresponsible
**4** 1 condense, contract   2 expand
   3 prehistoric   4 overestimate, overflow
**5** 1 condenses   2 expands   3 prehistoric
   4 overflowed   5 inconsistent   6 unlikely
   7 disagree

**6**

|   | sentence a | sentence b |
|---|---|---|
| 1 | expands | contracts |
| 2 | likely | unlikely |
| 3 | inaccurate | accurate |
| 4 | overestimated | underestimated |

### Exam practice

1 risk factors   2 impacts   3 sea levels
4 glaciers   5 to be expanding   6 unlikely to
7 drought   8 typhoons   9 global warming

## 10   Revision 1

### Revision exercises

**1** 1 My siblings are conventional.
   2 My colleagues are tolerant.
   3 People with violent spouses are often vulnerable.
   4 My employers are flexible.
   5 Our clients are idealistic.
**2** 1 c   2 d   3 a   4 b   5 e
**3** 1 d   2 f   3 b   4 c
**4** 1 b   2 b   3 a   4 b   5 a
**5** 1 b   2 c   3 b   4 a   5 c   6 a
**6** 1 d   2 e   3 c   4 a   5 b
**7** 1 True   2 False   3 True   4 True   5 False
**8** 1 attended   2 contemporary   3 organized
   4 broadcast   5 participate in   6 amateur
**9 Model answer**

Global warming has long been recognized as a serious problem by most climate scientists. Governments around the world have begun to take the necessary measures to address it. However, as our understanding of the scale and nature of the problem is still developing, efforts to tackle global warming need to be reassessed from time to time.

Recent evidence suggests that some risk factors associated with climate change may have been overstated. Sea levels are now expected to rise by approximately one metre, not two metres, as previously thought. This is because some glaciers and ice sheets appear to be contracting, the Arctic, for example, while others, such as the Antarctic, appear to be expanding. Also, it

is now thought that the Gulf Stream is unlikely to vanish. It may, therefore, be possible to scale back plans for flood defences in coastal areas.

However, there is also evidence that some of the consequences of climate change may have been understated. Tropical forests are now believed to be more vulnerable to drought. Hurricanes and typhoons may become more severe. Greater efforts should therefore be made to protect vulnerable populations, especially in tropical areas. Buildings in storm-prone areas may also need to be re-designed to withstand high winds.

These recommendations, however, address the symptoms of global warming, not the root cause: the generation of greenhouse gases. Whatever the precise scale and nature of the consequences of global warming, they are all undesirable. Clearly, more needs to be done to reduce the burning of fossil fuels. Stricter emissions targets should be set and use of alternative sources of energy encouraged. It would be profoundly irresponsible to do nothing about the causes of global warming.

## 11   Words for describing graphs and figures

### Practice exercises

**1** 1 d   2 a   3 c   4 g   5 f   6 e   7 b
**2** 1 c   2 d   3 f   4 e   5 b   6 a   7 g
**3**

| bar chart | diagram | flow chart | line graph |
|---|---|---|---|
| 2, 3, 4, 5, 9 | 1, 7 | 1, 8 | 4, 5, 9 |

| map | pie chart | table |
|---|---|---|
| 5, 7 | 5, 7 | 3, 6 |

**4** 1 flow chart, steps   2 map, key
   3 bar chart, vertical axis   4 diagram, arrows
   5 pie chart, segments   6 line graph, horizontal axis
   7 table, columns
**5** depicts   represents   compares
   illustrates   gives data

### Exam practice model answer

The charts show the percentage breakdown of government spending across nine categories in 2000 and 2010. Over the ten-year period, there were significant changes in expenditure.

In both years, the four largest areas of government expenditure were: education, healthcare, pensions, and defence, with education taking the largest share (24% in 2000 and 21% in 2010). The smallest areas of expenditure were transport, culture and leisure and 'other'. Interest on borrowing and spending on welfare lay in between.

Interestingly, between 2000 and 2010, spending on all four of the largest areas had dropped, with the exception of pensions, which remained the same at 19%. Spending on transport and culture and leisure also fell significantly, with the transport budget declining by two thirds. On the other hand, spending on welfare and interest on government borrowing rose markedly, with the latter doubling over the ten-year period to 10%.

Overall, the charts indicate that the government has had to cut expenditure in most areas in order to fund the cost of borrowing and welfare.

## 12 Words for describing change

### Practice exercises

**1** 1 c  2 a  3 e  4 f  5 b  6 d
**2** a –  b 0  c –  d +  e +  f 0
**3** year, decade, generation, century, millennium
**4**

| word | connotation | time expression |
|------|-------------|-----------------|
| **1** alter | 0 | five centuries ago |
| **2** diminish | – | the last few years |
| **3** refine | + | over the next decade |
| **4** shift | 0 | within a generation |
| **5** transform | + | the next millennium |

## 13 Words expressing similarity and difference

### Practice exercises

**1** Circle: a, b, g, h     Underline: c, d, e, f
**2** 1 identical  2 alike  3 diverse  4 distinct
 5 equivalent  6 contrary  7 conversely
 8 comparable
**3** 1 differ  2 identical
**4** 1/2 differentiate/distinguish  3 differs
 4 identical  5/6 similar/analogous
**5**

| verb | noun |
|------|------|
| compare | comparison |
| contrast | contrast |
| differ | difference |
| resemble | resemblance |
| vary | variety |

| adjective | adverb |
|-----------|--------|
| comparable | comparably |
| contrasting | contrastingly |
| different | differently |
| × | × |
| varied/variable | variably |

**6** Circle: varied, comparable, comparison, resemblance, differently, contrast (noun), contrast (verb)
**7** 1 varied  2 comparable  3 comparison
 4 resemblance  5 differently  6 contrast
 7 contrasted

### Exam practice

1 identical  2 different  3 comparable
4 different  5 alike

## 14 Words describing cause and effect

### Practice exercises

**1** 1 the growth of social networking
  [a reduction of government control of information]
 2 tax rises
  [a slowdown in investment]
 3 [Better maternal health]
  the government's reform of services
 4 The collapse of the bank
  [financial crises throughout the country]
 5 [The company's insolvency]
  a series of poor decisions made five years ago
 6 His statements about corruption in the police
  [an immediate response]
**2** 1 whereas, complete  **d** an antonym
  (cropped = reduced/cut)
 2 devices which reduce pollution generated by cars
  **c** a definition
  (a catalytic converter = a device which reduces pollution generated by cars)
 3 weapons  **a** a superordinate term
  (a grenade = a type of weapon)
 4 for example failing to adequately consider...
  **b** an example
  (flawed = faulty)
**3** 1 b  2 a  3 b  4 a  5 a  6 a  7 b  8 b  9 a

### Exam practice

1 B  2 A  3 C  4 B  5 D

## 15 Signposting expressions for writing

### Practice exercises

**1** 1 e  2 f  3 b  4 c  5 a  6 d
**2** 1 b  2 b and c  3 a  4 b  5 c  6 d
**3** 1 prior  2 nevertheless  3 on balance
  4 subsequent  5 whereas  6 respectively
**4** 1 Nevertheless  2 initial  3 subsequent
  4 moreover  5 former  6 whereas *OR* whilst

### Exam practice model answer

Studying abroad has become increasingly common in the last few years, especially for young people from countries such as China and India. Many students and their families clearly consider the experience worth the sacrifices involved. **The former** often give up friendships when they move abroad; **the latter** often use their life savings. **Moreover,** many governments are willing to invest huge sums of money in sponsoring their young people to study in universities overseas. However, this trend has drawbacks as well as benefits for those concerned.

One potential drawback is that the instruction international students receive may not be relevant to their home contexts. For example, students from developing countries who go to Western countries for teacher training are often taught to use teaching techniques that are suitable for small classes. When they return home they are often expected to teach classes of 40 or 50 students . **Hence,** what they have been trained to do may not be relevant.

Another potential drawback is the phenomenon of 'brain drain'. **Prior** to leaving home, they may be fully committed to returning. **Nevertheless,** students are often at the stage in their lives when they are forming their most important personal and professional relationships. **Thus** they may choose to remain in the host country on completing their studies.

However, most international students find ways of making the experience work well for themselves and others involved. Most return home, enriched by new friendships made abroad. **Furthermore,** most find ways of adapting what they have learned to their home context. **On balance,** the drawbacks do not outweigh the benefits.

## 16 Adverbs

### Practice exercises

**1** Underline: provisionally, relatively, approximately, ideally, indefinitely, particularly, necessarily
**2** 1 particularly  2 ideally  3 provisionally
  4 indefinitely  5 necessarily  6 approximately
  7 relatively
**3** 1 f  2 c  3 a  4 e  5 g  6 b  7 d
**4** 1 absol[u]tely  2 necess[a]rily
  3 part[i]cularly  4 pres[u]mably
  5 supp[o]sedly  6 surpr[i]singly

### Exam practice sample answer

Examiner: Hello. My name is Susan Davie. Can you tell me your full name, please?
Student: Anna Delgado
Examiner: Thanks. Can I please see your identification?... Thanks, that's great. I'm going to ask you some questions about yourself now. Tell me about your favourite film or television programme.
Student: A television programme I particularly like is a comedy about people who work in an office. It looks quite ordinary on the surface, but the characters are very funny. If you've ever worked in an office, you would understand the humour.
Examiner: How do you think television has changed since you were a child?
Student: There are a lot more television channels, so, supposedly, there is a lot more choice. But in fact many of the programmes today are very similar. In the past there were fewer programmes but more variety.
Examiner: Are there any types of programmes that you don't like to watch?
Student: Absolutely. I really don't like soap operas. I find the story lines completely unrealistic and I can never keep track of all the different characters and how they're related.
Examiner: I'd like to ask you a few questions about transport. How do normally travel to your work or place of study?
Student: I usually walk to work as my workplace is only two kilometres from my home. It takes me approximately 25 minutes to get there. However, if the weather is bad, I get a lift from my brother or my sister-in law.

Examiner: How do people in your country normally travel?

Student: More and more people own a car, so, inevitably, most people travel by car. Unfortunately, it's not the healthiest or most environmentally friendly mode of travel, but it is convenient.

Examiner: How easy is it to get around in your country?

Student: It's relatively easy to get around, especially by car. The road network is extensive and generally in a good state of repair. The exception is in the mountainous areas in the west, where the roads are comparatively rough and narrow.

Examiner: We're now going to talk about places of interest in your country. What do you think is the most interesting building or monument in your country?

Student: Undoubtedly, the national museum. It was once a palace but it now houses the national art collection. It was built approximately 400 years ago and each room has a particular theme. My favourite room is designed around the theme of music and holds the museum's collection of musical instruments.

Examiner: Do you prefer historic building styles to modern architecture?

Student: Not necessarily. I think there are a lot of interesting buildings being built these days. I like the way glass and steel can be used to create light airy spaces.

Examiner: To what extent do people in your country value traditional architecture?

Student: Generally speaking, people still prefer traditional architecture and the government has promoted the conservation of historic buildings. Not surprisingly, it's very difficult to get permission to alter a traditional structure or construct a modern building in an old area.

## 17 Words for problems and solutions

1  1 c  2 b  3 a  4 d
2  1 b  2 c  3 e  4 a  5 e
3  1 repaired  2 alleviate  3 resolve
   4 tackle  5 resolve
4  1 damage  2 address  3 tackle
   4 question  5 complication  6 alleviate

5  adjusting  different  foreign  referred
   adjustment  acceptance  environment
   approaching  alleviated

### Exam practice

1  student welfare
2  letter of enrolment
3  damage to property
4  intervene (if necessary)
5  welfare handbook

## 18 Words for talking about ideas

### Practice exercises

1  1 d  2 h  3 g  4 b  5 f  6 c  7 a  8 e
2  Underline: 3 , 4, 6
   Circle:  1, 2, 5
3  1 d  2 c  3 a  4 b
4

| noun | ambiguity | bias | concept |
|---|---|---|---|
| adjective | ambiguous | biased | conceptual |
| noun | credibility | dogma | validity |
| adjective | credible | dogmatic | valid |

5  1 framework   2 validity
   3 perspective   4 flaws

### Exam practice

1 philosophers and psychologists (any order)
2 consensus
3 theories
4 relief and incongruity (any order)
5 misfortune or inferiority (any order)
6 valid

## 19 Emphasis and understatement

### Practice exercises

1  Circle: 1 abundant   3 ample   4 marked
   Underline: 2 negligible   5 modest
2  1 definitive   2 undisputed   3 confirmed
   4 will   5 known to be
3  Cross out: 1 b   2 c   3 a   4 c   5 c   6 c
4  1 liable to   2 marked   3 marginally
   4 seldom   5 definitive

## Exam practice

### Model answer

The graph shows the number of hours per day on average that children spent watching television. The graph covers the period between 1950 and 2010.

From 1950 to 1960, there was a modest rise in the average number of hours children spent in front of the television set. This was followed by a marked increase from approximately one hour to four hours of viewing per day among children between 1965 and 1985. Over the next five years, there was a decrease. However this trend proved negligible as the viewing figure then rose again marginally. Between 2010 and 2011, there was another modest decline in the hours children spent watching television.

Overall, there has been a significant rise in television viewing over the sixty-year period, though there is some indication that this trend may be changing.

# 20  Revision 2

## Practice exercises

**1** 1 graph   2 vertical   3 horizontal

### Model answer

Overall, the graph indicates that there were greater fluctuations in gym membership among men than among women. The number of male members started the period at just over two thousand and reached highs of four thousand in 1985 and five thousand around 2005. The lowest rates were between 1993 and 1997 and more recently in 2010 when the rate dipped as low as one thousand.

Female gym membership began lower at one thousand, doubled by 1984, and then fluctuated between two and three thousand for the remainder of the period. When male rates were at their lowest, female rates were higher. This was particularly true between 1993 and 1997 when over three thousand women held gym membership.

In brief, there were marked differences in rates of male and female gym memberships in the period covered.

**2** 1 decline   2 abandoning   3 evolved
   4 four decades   5 hardly altered
   6 a generation ago
**3** 1 distinguish   2 identical   3 equivalent
   4 varies   5 conversely   6 diverse   7 comparable
**4** 1 cause   2 cause   3 consequence   4 cause
   5 consequence   6 consequence   7 cause
**5** 1 She knew she did not have the right qualifications; nevertheless, she applied for the job.
   2 Geography is the study of the countries of the world, whereas, geology is the study of the structure and origin of the earth.
   3 Over the last ten years, there has been a marked divergence in the salaries of executives and the salaries of ordinary workers; the former has increased by one hundred and eighty-seven per cent, while the latter has increased by only twenty-seven per cent.
   4 Shopkeepers should be penalized if they sell cigarettes to young people; moreover, the minimum age at which young people can legally buy tobacco products should be increased to eighteen.
   5 In many countries, it is very difficult to train for a new career after the age of forty; hence, people need to think carefully before choosing an occupation.
   6 Prior to the dispute over land ownership, the two communities had lived harmoniously for many years.
**6** 1 False   2 True   3 False   4 True
   5 False   6 True   7 False
**8** 1 notion   2 credibility   3 valid   4 conjecture
   5 compelling   6 biased
**9** 1 b   2 a   3 a   4 a   5 b   6 b

# Collocations

These are common collocations for the vocabulary presented in the units.

## Unit 1

### People and relationships:
**client**
a **firm's** clients
**advise/represent** a client
a **prospective** client

**parent**
the parents **of** someone
a **foster/adoptive/birth/single/lone** parent

**sibling**
a **younger/elder** sibling
sibling **rivalry**

### Adjectives to describe people:
**autonomous**
an autonomous **individual**
an autonomous **region/republic/province/unit**
**fiercely/relatively/largely** autonomous

**consistent**
a consistent **player/performer**
consistent **with** something
consistent with a **finding/hypothesis**
**entirely/fairly/broadly/remarkably** consistent

**conventional**
conventional **wisdom/thinking/treatment/
  methods**
conventional **forces/weapons**

**co-operative**
a co-operative **approach/effort/relationship**

**efficient**
an efficient **use** of something
an efficient **way** of doing something
an efficient **manner**
**highly/extremely** efficient
**fuel/energy** efficient

**flexible**
a flexible **approach/system/arrangement**
flexible **working/working hours**
a flexible **rate/market**

**idealistic**
an idealistic **notion/vision/view**

**tolerant**
tolerant **of** something
a tolerant **society/country/attitude**
**racially** tolerant

**vulnerable**
vulnerable **to** something
vulnerable to **attack/damage/fire**
vulnerable **children/women/people**
a vulnerable **position**
**especially/highly/increasingly** vulnerable

## Unit 2

### Health problems:
**addiction**
addiction **to** something
**drug/heroin/cocaine/nicotine/alcohol** addiction
a **long-term/chronic/serious** addiction
**cure/treat/overcome/fight against/feed**
   an addiction
an addiction **problem/clinic/counsellor**

**allergy**
an allergy **to** something
**develop/diagnose/treat/trigger/cause**
   an allergy
a **severe/common/serious/
   life-threatening** allergy
a **food/peanut/penicillin/skin** allergy
allergy **sufferers/symptoms**

**dehydration**
**avoid/prevent/cause/suffer** from dehydration
**severe/mild/extreme** dehydration

**disease**
a **fatal/deadly/chronic** disease
**heart/lung/kidney** disease
**transmit/contract/develop** a disease
**prevent/treat/cure/fight** a disease
**diagnose/spread/cause** a disease

**infection**
a **viral/bacterial/urinary/respiratory** infection
a **chest/ear/lung** infection

contract/transmit/**spread** an infection
**prevent/combat/fight/treat/cure/**
   **detect** an infection
infection **control/prevention**

### obesity
**tackle/prevent/fight/reduce/cause** obesity
the obesity **epidemic/rate/problem**
**childhood/child/adult** obesity
**morbid/extreme/severe** obesity

### stroke
a **suspected/minor/severe/fatal/mini** stroke
a stroke **victim/patient/unit**
**suffer/have/prevent** a stroke

## Verbs associated with treatment:
### administer
administered **by** someone/something
administer something **to** someone
administer a **dose/injection/vaccine/drug**
administer **medication/antibiotics/morphine**
**orally/intravenously** administered

### diagnose
someone is diagnosed **with** something
someone/something is diagnosed **as** something
diagnosed with **cancer/diabetes/leukaemia**
diagnosed with a **disorder/disease/tumour**
diagnosed as **epileptic/diabetic**

### examine
a **doctor/psychiatrist/specialist**
   examines someone
examine a **patient**
examine someone **carefully**
examined **by** someone

### screen
screen **for** something
screen for a **disease/abnormality/condition**
screen for **TB/diabetes/cancer**
screen a **patient/donor**
**routinely/properly** screen

### vaccinate
vaccinated **against** something
vaccinated against **smallpox/measles/**
   **flu/rabies**
**fully** vaccinated
**children/adults/animals** are vaccinated
**have** someone vaccinated

# Unit 3

## Academic subjects:
### archaeology
an archaeology **student/professor/**
   **lecturer/department**
**maritime/biblical/industrial/classical**
   archaeology

### astronomy
an astronomy **professor/enthusiast/**
   **mission**
**planetary/optical/theoretical/modern**
   astronomy

### economics
an economics **professor/degree/department**
**Keynesian/classical/experimental/**
   **free-market** economics
**development/market** economics

### geology
the geology **of** somewhere
the geology of the **area/region/island/earth**

### linguistics
**modern/historical/applied** linguistics

### psychology
**educational/evolutionary** psychology
**clinical/cognitive** psychology

### sociology
the sociology **of** something
the sociology of **religion/science**
a sociology **professor/lecturer/department/student**

## Academic activities:
### analyse
analyse **data/statistics/results/trends**
analyse a **sample**
analyse something **critically/**
   **carefully/scientifically**

### claim
claim **falsely/rightly/wrongly/repeatedly**
a **true/false** claim

### define
define something **as/in terms of** something
define a **term/concept**
a **rule/law** defines something
**clearly/narrowly/broadly** defined

## evaluate
evaluate a **situation/impact/risk**
evaluate the **effectiveness** of something
evaluate the **performance** of someone
**carefully** evaluate something

## investigate
investigate a **link/case/incident/complaint/
   allegation**
**thoroughly/fully/properly** investigate

## Nouns associated with research:
### evidence
evidence **of/for** something
**find/gather/collect** evidence
**present/produce** evidence
evidence **suggests/shows**
**clear/strong/conclusive** evidence

### hypothesis
**test/support/confirm/propose** a hypothesis
a **null/testable/alternative** hypothesis

### theory
a theory **of** something
the theory of **evolution/relativity**
**develop/propose/formulate/test/
   prove/apply** a theory
a **scientific/**an **evolutionary** theory

# Unit 4

## Verbs associated with travel and adventure:
### accompany
accompanied **by** someone
accompanied by a **bodyguard/adult/escort**
accompany a **text/illustration/article**

### delay
delay the **onset/start** of something

### encounter
encounter **resistance/opposition**
encounter a **difficulty/problem**

### overcome
overcome a **problem/difficulty/
   injury/deficit/obstacle**

### seek
seek something **from** someone
be sought **for** something

seek **help/advice/refuge/treatment**
seek **approval/permission/compensation**
**actively/eagerly/urgently/desperately/
   unsuccessfully** seek

## Nouns associated with travel and adventure:
### challenge
**present/pose/accept/face/meet** a challenge
a **serious/real/major/great** challenge
a **legal** challenge

### destination
a **tourist/holiday/travel/popular/
   favourite** destination
a **final/ultimate** destination

### route
a route **to/from** somewhere
**take/follow/choose/travel** a route
a **main/direct/circuitous/alternative/
   scenic** route
a **trade/escape/supply/bus** route
a route **map/network**

## Adjectives to describe experiences:
### intense
intense **heat/pain/pressure/scrutiny/
   fighting**
intense **debate/speculation/negotiations**
intense **competition/rivalry**

### pivotal
pivotal **in** something
a pivotal **role/moment/figure/point/
   position**
**potentially/absolutely** pivotal
**prove/become** pivotal

### profound
a profound **sense** of something
a profound **change/impact/effect/
   influence/implication**
profound **shock/sadness**

### valuable
**extremely/less/very** valuable
**prove/become** valuable
a valuable **asset/lesson/resource/
   experience**
a valuable **contribution/item**
valuable **property/information/advice**

# Unit 5

## Nouns to describe dimensions:
**angle**
a **90-degree/45-degree/acute** angle

**circumference**
the circumference **of** something
**in** circumference
**measure** the circumference

**diameter**
a diameter **of** x cm
x cm **in** diameter

**height**
a height **of** x
**have/reach** a height of x
of **medium/normal/average** height
the **maximum/minimum** height
the **average** height

**length**
the length **of** something
something **stretches/extends** the length of
    something
**have** a length of x
**measure/run/walk/travel** the length of
    something
the **entire/full/whole/total/overall**
    length of something

**radius**
a radius **of/around** something
**in/within** a radius of something
a **50-mile/ten-mile/1km** radius
a radius of x
the radius of a circle

**volume**
the volume of **traffic/shares/data**
**export/sales/traffic** volume
the **average/total/estimated** volume
the **sheer/huge/high** volume
**increase/reduce** volume

**width**
the width **of** something
an amount **in** width
a width of x **feet/inches/metres/miles**
**adjust/vary/decrease/increase/extend**
    the width

the **full/overall/approximate/**
    **minimum/maximum** width

## Actions:
**adjust**
adjust **to** something
adjusted **for** something
adjust **figures/rates**
adjust something to **reflect/fit** something
**seasonally/periodically/automatically/**
    **manually** adjusted

**convey**
convey a **sense/impression** of something
convey the **meaning** of something
convey something **vividly/powerfully/accurately**
convey **information/emotion**
convey a **message**

**launch**
launch a **product/model/brand/book/magazine/car**
the launch **of** something
a **product/book** launch
an **official** launch
**announce/delay/postpone** a launch

**reinforce**
reinforce a **perception/view/impression/belief**
**mutually/powerfully/constantly/**
    **further** reinforce something
reinforce a **notion/message/stereotype**
**powerfully/further** reinforce something

**secure**
secure a **victory/conviction/place/win/deal**
secure the **approval/support/backing** of someone
secure **funding/peace**

**suspend**
suspend something **until** a time
**immediately/temporarily/indefinitely**
    suspend something
suspended from a **ceiling/rafter/hook**
suspended by **wire/rope**

# Unit 6

## Nouns associated with human geography
**commuter**
a commuter **train/plane/bus**
a commuter **town/belt**

**congestion**
**traffic/road/airport** congestion
**cause/increase** congestion
**reduce/ease** congestion
congestion **charge/charging**

**resident**
residents **of/in** somewhere
**evacuate/warn/advise** residents
residents **say/fear/complain about/want/
   report** something
**former/local/permanent/nearby/elderly**
   residents

**immigrant**
a **skilled/illegal** immigrant
a **first-generation/second-generation**
   immigrant
**deport/detain/smuggle** immigrants
immigrants **arrive/settle/flee**
an immigrant **population/community/
   worker/visa**

**infrastructure**
the infrastructure **of** something
**have** infrastructure in place
**build/rebuild/improve/destroy** infrastructure
**existing/basic** infrastructure
**transport/rail/telecommunications/security**
   infrastructure

**inhabitant**
the inhabitants **of** somewhere
**indigenous/native/original/local** inhabitants

**neighbourhood**
a **safe/good/bad/poor/quiet** neighbourhood
a **residential/run-down** neighbourhood

**Adjectives:**
**pioneering**
pioneering **work/surgery/research**
a pioneering **technique/concept/study**
a pioneering **surgeon/conservationist/geologist**

**historic**
a historic **agreement/decision/victory**
a historic **achievement/opportunity**
a historic **event/occasion/moment**

**rural**
a rural **area/community/population**
a rural **economy/development/road**

**urban**
urban **sprawl/renewal/regeneration/
   planning**
an urban **neighbourhood/environment**
urban **warfare/poverty/living**

# Unit 7

## Reporting verbs:
**advocate**
advocated **by** someone
advocate **reform/legislation/violence**
**openly/strongly/publicly** advocate

**acknowledge**
acknowledge the **existence/
   importance** of something
acknowledge the **need** for something
acknowledge **difficulties**
**publicly/readily** acknowledge
**widely/universally** acknowledged

**dispute**
dispute a **claim/assertion/allegation**
dispute **figures/facts**
**hotly/vigorously/bitterly** disputed

**justify**
justified **by** something
**entirely/wholly/amply** justified
**morally/ethically/rationally/economically/
   scientifically** justified
justify a **war/invasion/action/expense**

**object**
object **to** something
object to the **idea/notion/use**
object **strongly**

**question**
question the **validity/legality** of something
question the **wisdom/motives/integrity**
   of something/someone

**suggest**
**evidence/research** suggests
**data/findings** suggest something
a **poll/study/report/study** suggests
   something
**strongly/tentatively** suggest
suggest **otherwise**

## Nouns associated with persuasion:
**benefit**
the benefit **of** something
**health/economic/financial/social** benefit
**reap** the benefit of something

**debate**
a debate **on/over/about/within** something
a **heated/lively/intense/ongoing** debate
**spark/provoke/trigger** a debate

**drawback**
**have** drawbacks
**outweigh/overcome** drawbacks
the **main/only** drawback
a **big/major** drawback

**proof**
proof **of** something
proof of **identity/residency**
**conclusive/definite/irrefutable/further/
   concrete** proof
**need/provide/offer/furnish** proof

## People who persuade:
**politician**
a **democratic/conservative/liberal/
   opposition** politician
a **leading/senior/prominent/local/
   corrupt** politician
**elect** a politician
politicians **promise/claim/decide** things

# Unit 8

## Nouns for cultural interests:
**current affairs**
a current affairs **programme**

**drama**
**be** in a drama
**watch** a drama
a drama is **set/filmed** somewhere
a drama is **based on** something
a drama **continues/begins/unfolds**

**opera**
an opera **about** something
an opera **singer/house**

**orchestra**
a **chamber/symphony** orchestra
**conduct** an orchestra
an orchestra **plays/performs** something

**poetry**
**write/compose/publish** poetry
**recite/read/quote** poetry
**love/lyric/war/epic** poetry
a poetry **book/anthology**

## Adjectives:
**classical**
classical **music/ballet**
classical **tradition**
classical **architecture/mythology/civilization**
the classical **world**

## Verbs associated with involvement:
**assemble**
assemble **in/at** somewhere
assemble **for** something
assemble for a **meeting/ceremony/occasion**
a **crowd/team** assembles
**delegates/guests/workers** assemble

**attend**
attended **by** someone
attend a **meeting/conference/summit/funeral**
**delegates/guests/representatives**
   attend something
**sparsely/poorly/well** attended
attend **regularly/rarely**

**broadcast**
broadcast **on** something
broadcast on **television/radio**
broadcast **live**
broadcast a **message/programme/image**
a broadcasting **network**

**establish**
establish a **link/relationship**
**firmly/quickly** establish something

**observe**
**scientists/researchers** observe something
observe **behaviour**
**closely** observe

**organize**
organize things **by/into** something
organize things by **group/topic**
organize things into **units/sections/chapters**
organize a **meeting/conference/event/
   demonstration**
**well/poorly/highly** organized

**participate**

participate **in** something

participate in a **discussion/activity/debate/process**

participate **equally/willingly/effectively**

# Unit 9

## Natural processes:
**condense**

condense **into/out of** something

condense into **rain/liquid/droplets**

**vapour/moisture/steam/gas** condenses

a **cloud** condenses

**contract**

the **throat** contracts

the **muscles/ventricles** contract

contract **rhythmically/rapidly**

**expand**

expanded **by** an amount

an expanding **universe/economy/population**

expand **capacity/coverage/production**

expand the **scope/range** of something

expand **rapidly/dramatically**

**flow**

flow **into** a place

**water/blood** flows

a **current** flows

flow **freely**

a **steady/constant/free** flow

## Verbs associated with scientific study:
**estimate**

estimate something **at** x

estimate **cost/value/revenue**

an estimated **percentage/amount**

**predict**

predict an **event/outcome**

predict a **fall/drop/decline/rise/recovery/upturn**

a **forecaster/economist/analyst** predicts something

predict something **accurately/confidently/correctly**

**impossible/difficult/possible** to predict

**state**

state a **fact/reason/preference**

state **clearly/explicitly/categorically/unequivocally**

state **repeatedly/incorrectly/publicly**

a **letter/document/report/rule/article** states something

## Adjectives:
**accurate**

**reasonably/historically/scientifically/factually** accurate

accurate **information/figures**

an accurate **description/measurement/diagnosis/prediction**

**likely**

likely to **become/remain/continue/happen/cause**

**be/seem/look/appear/become** likely

**more/most/very/highly/increasingly** likely

**less/as/not/also/quite** likely

a likely **target/explanation/outcome/candidate**

## Nouns associated with climate:
**current**

a current **of** something

a current of **air/electricity**

a **strong/ocean** current

**drought**

a **prolonged/severe/devastating** drought

drought **affects/hits/devastates** somewhere

drought **conditions**

**flood**

a **bad/devastating/flash** flood

a flood **hits/sweeps** somewhere

**glacier**

an **Antarctic/Alaskan** glacier

a glacier **melts/retreats/moves**

**hurricane**

a **devastating/deadly/major/powerful** hurricane

**withstand/predict** a hurricane

a hurricane **hits/destroys/damages** something

**typhoon**

a **powerful/deadly** typhoon

# Unit 11

## Nouns for graphs and figures:
**bar chart**

a bar chart **shows/illustrates/reflects** something

a bar chart **compares** things

**diagram**

a diagram **illustrates/shows** something

**draw** a diagram

a **schematic/explanatory/simple/
  complex** diagram

**pie chart**
a pie chart **shows/indicates/displays** something

## Components of graphs and figures:
**row**
a row **of** things
**in/into** a row
**put/place/arrange** things in a row
the **front/back/top/bottom** row
a **single/double** row

**segment**
a segment **of** something
a segment of a **circle/pie chart**
a segment of a **market/industry**
a **fast-growing/mid-sized/profitable** segment

**stage**
a stage **of** something
a stage of **development/evolution/pregnancy**
a stage of a **competition/tournament**
a stage of a **cycle/process**

## Verbs meaning 'show':
**depict**
depicted **as/in** something
a **painting/photograph** depicts something
a **mural/fresco/cartoon** depicts something
depict a **scene/landscape/character**
**graphically/vividly/accurately** depicted

**represent**
represent a **difference/increase/shift/step**

# Unit 12

## Verbs associated with change:
**abandon**
abandon a **child/baby/project/plan/idea**
abandon an **attempt/effort**
an abandoned **building/warehouse/
  mine/quarry/vehicle/car**
**hastily/abruptly/temporarily**
  abandon someone/something

**adjust**
adjust **to** something
adjusted **for** something
adjust **figures/rates**

adjust something to **reflect/fit** something
**seasonally/periodically/automatically/
  manually** adjusted

**alter**
alter the **course/outcome** of something
alter the **composition/balance/
  structure** of something
alter the **facts/perceptions/wording**
**radically/fundamentally/structurally/
  genetically** alter something

**decline**
decline **from** x **to** y
decline **by** x
**steadily/rapidly/sharply** decline

**develop**
develop **into** something
develop something **further**
develop a **technique/strategy/idea**
develop a **business/product**
develop **rapidly/quickly**

**diminish**
diminish **in** something
diminish in **importance/size/number**
**rapidly/gradually** diminish
**greatly/drastically/considerably** diminished

**evolve**
evolve **from/into** something
evolve **over** time
**culture/language/society/technology** evolves
**humans/organisms/species** evolve
**rapidly/constantly/gradually/slowly** evolve

**modify**
modify **food/crops/ingredients**
**genetically/chemically** modified
**extensively/significantly** modified

**refine**
refine **oil/uranium/gasoline/sugar**
refine a **technique/procedure/skill**
**continually/constantly/greatly** refine something

**shift**
shift **uncomfortably/restlessly/uneasily**
shift one's **weight/position**
shift the **focus/emphasis/balance**

**transform**
transform something **from/into** something
**completely/magically/dramatically** transform

transform **society**
transform a **country/business/area**
transform the **economy/landscape/country/world**

## Nouns for periods of time:
**century**
centuries **of** something

**decade**
the **last/next** decade
**recent/past/previous** decades
a decade **later/earlier/ago**
decades **of** something
decades of **war/conflict/neglect**

**millennium**
**celebrate/approach/reach** the millennium
a **new/next/second/third** millennium

# Unit 13

## Verbs for describing difference:
**contrast**
contrast a **view/approach** with something
contrast **sharply/starkly**

**differ**
differ **from** something
differ **significantly/considerably/widely/
   sharply/markedly**
**opinions/views** differ

**differentiate**
differentiate **between** things
differentiate something **from** something
a differentiated **product/brand**
a differentiating **factor**

**distinguish**
distinguish **between** things
distinguish something **from** something
**reliably/easily/clearly** distinguish

**vary**
vary **from** something
vary from **region to region/person to person**
vary **considerably/enormously/greatly/widely**
**opinions/prices/estimates/practices** vary
varying **degrees/sizes/lengths/amounts**

## Verbs for describing similarity:
**compare**
compare something **with/to** something

**resemble**
**closely/somewhat/strongly** resemble something

## Adjectives and adverbs for describing difference:
**contrary**
contrary **to** something
**run/seem** contrary to something
a contrary **view/opinion/direction**
contrary **evidence/information**

**distinct**
distinct **from** something
a distinct **category/type/species/entity**

**diverse**
**ethnically/culturally** diverse
**geographically/linguistically** diverse
diverse **backgrounds**
a diverse **group/range/population/society**

## Adjectives for describing similarity:
**alike**
**look/sound** alike
**dress/think** alike

**analogous**
analogous **to** something
a **manner/situation/process/position** is analogous
**somewhat/closely/roughly/directly** analogous

**equivalent**
the equivalent **of** something
the equivalent of a **pound/pint**
a **modern/modern-day** equivalent
a **cinematic/literary/musical/visual** equivalent
the **male/female** equivalent

**identical**
identical **to/with** something
an identical **copy/score/twin**
identical **wording/circumstances**
**functionally/genetically** identical
**look** identical

# Unit 14

## Nouns:
**chain reaction**
a chain reaction **of** things
a chain reaction of **events/damage/explosions**
**cause/set off/trigger/initiate** a chain reaction
a chain reaction **occurs**

## consequence

the consequences of **war/action/failure**

the consequences for the **economy/future/ region**

**suffer/face/accept/consider/ understand** the consequences

**serious/severe/tragic** consequences

**likely/unintended** consequences

## impact

an impact on the **environment/economy**

an impact on **society/health/earnings/tourism**

a **significant/important/major/profound** impact

a **lasting/immediate/negative/ adverse/positive** impact

## influence

the influence of **alcohol/drugs**

**have/exert** influence on someone/something

**considerable/powerful/positive/political** influence

a **major/important/strong/good/bad** influence

## outcome

the outcome **of** something

**await/predict/decide/affect/influence** the outcome

the **likely** outcome

a **successful** outcome

## repercussion

**serious/possible/potential/negative** repercussions

**have/suffer/fear** repercussions

## Verbs:

### affect

**badly/adversely/directly** affect

**seriously/severely/greatly** affect

affect the **outcome/quality/ performance** of something

affect **people/everyone**

### contribute

contribute **to** something

a contributing **factor**

contribute **greatly/directly/ significantly/substantially**

### determine

determined **by** something

determine something's **outcome/fate/ future/value**

**genetically/biologically** determined

determine the **cause/extent** of something

determine **precisely/conclusively/exactly**

## generate

generated **by** something

generate **excitement/publicity/ controversy/enthusiasm**

generate **wealth/income/profit**

generate **electricity/energy/heat/power**

## induce

induce a **state/feeling/sense/change**

induce a **response/reaction/heart attack/coma**

induce **sleep/vomiting/fear/panic/relaxation**

## provoke

provoke **outrage/fury/controversy/fury/anger**

provoke a **reaction/response/ backlash/outcry/debate**

## result

result in **death/arrest**

result in a **loss/reduction/increase**

result from **use/exposure**

result from a **failure/lack**

## stem

stem **from** something

a **problem** stems from something

stem from a **fact/incident/belief/misconception**

stem the **tide/flow/spread** of something

## trigger

trigger a **response/reaction/change**

trigger a **crisis/attack/war/debate**

trigger a **tsunami/landslide/avalanche**

# Unit 15

## Referring to sequence:

### initial

an initial **reaction/response/impression/diagnosis**

an initial **offering/purchase/investment/meeting**

the initial **stages/results/success**

### latter

**choose/prefer** the latter

the latter **stage/part/category**

### prior

prior **approval/permission/consent/agreement**

prior **knowledge/experience**

a prior **engagement/arrangement**

the prior **period/week/month/year**

a **day/hour/week/month/year** prior to something

**subsequent**

a subsequent **year/event/period/generation**

a subsequent **investigation/inquiry/purchase**

## Generalising:
**overall**

overall **spending/revenue**

an overall **impression/strategy/performance**

an overall **majority/increase**

# Unit 16

**comparatively**

comparatively **little/small**

comparatively **rare/modest/mild/inexpensive**

**indefinitely**

**continue** indefinitely

be **suspended/postponed/delayed/
closed** indefinitely

be **held/detained** indefinitely

**inevitably**

inevitably **result in/lead to/mean** something

**particularly**

particularly **in/among** something

particularly **useful/important/interesting/
relevant**

particularly **vulnerable/sensitive/difficult**

particularly **concerned/pleased/impressed**

**provisionally**

provisionally **agreed/accepted/scheduled**

provisionally **entitled/titled**

**relatively**

relatively **small/low/short/easy/simple**

relatively **easily/cheaply/recently/little**

# Unit 17

## Nouns for problems:
**crisis**

a **political/economic/humanitarian/
financial** crisis

a **severe** crisis

a **hostage/energy/health/cash** crisis

**resolve/face** a crisis

a crisis **point/situation/meeting**

**dilemma**

**pose/raise/face/solve** a dilemma

a **moral/ethical/policy/workplace** dilemma

## Verbs associated with problems:
**damage**

damage a **building/vehicle**

damage the **environment**

damage someone's **brain/ligaments/
knee/ankle**

damage someone's **prospects/
reputation/credibility**

**badly/severely/seriously/permanently**
damage something

**deteriorate**

deteriorate **into** something

a **condition/situation** deteriorates

someone's **health** deteriorates

a deteriorating **situation/condition**

**quickly/rapidly/sharply/steadily** deteriorate

**exacerbate**

exacerbated **by** something

exacerbate a **problem/situation/conflict/
crisis**

exacerbate **tensions/symptoms**

## Verbs associated with solutions:
**address**

address a **problem/issue/concern/question**

**adequately/urgently/specifically/directly**
address something

**eradicate**

eradicate something **in/from** a place

**virtually/completely/almost** eradicated

eradicate **disease/poverty/illiteracy/racism**

**intervene**

intervene **in** something

intervene **personally/directly**

intervene in a **dispute/conflict/war/row/crisis**

intervene in a **case/affair/matter/situation/
process**

**resolve**

**quickly/peacefully/amicably** resolve something

resolve a **dispute/conflict/crisis/issue/problem**

**tackle**

tackle a **problem/issue/task/crisis**

tackle **crime/poverty/corruption**

# Unit 18

## Nouns for ideas:
**concept**
the concept of **freedom/democracy/justice**
**understand/introduce/explain** a concept
a **basic/original/abstract/simple/**
  **key/underlying** concept
a **marketing/design** concept

**conjecture**
a matter **of/for** conjecture
conjecture **about** something
**fuel/spark/prompt** conjecture
**scientific/historical** conjecture

**consensus**
the consensus **amongst** people
a consensus **on/about** something
**reach/build/achieve** a consensus
**seek/establish** a consensus
a **scientific/cross-party/broad/general**
  consensus

**dogma**
**accept/question/challenge** dogma
**ideological/religious/outdated** dogma

**framework**
**within** a framework
a framework **of/for** something
**agree/develop/establish/set** a framework
a **legal/regulatory/legislative/political**
  framework
a **conceptual/theoretical** framework

**ideology**
the ideology **of** something
**embrace/reject** an ideology
an ideology **influences/motivates/**
  **drives** someone
a **political/religious/secular/economic** ideology

**model**
a model **of** something
a model of **efficiency/consistency/excellence**
**introduce/adopt/follow** a model
a model of **evolution**
**propose** a model

**perspective**
a perspective **on** something
the perspective **of** someone

**from** the perspective of someone/something
a **historical/feminist/sociological** perspective
a **different/new/fresh** perspective

**stance**
someone's stance **towards/on** something
**adopt/maintain/take/assume** a stance
a **neutral/tough/aggressive/moral** stance

## Adjectives for describing ideas:
**ambiguous**
**deliberately/somewhat/highly** ambiguous
**remain/seem** ambiguous
an ambiguous **relationship/position/**
  **result/phrase/statement**
ambiguous **language/wording**

**biased**
biased **against** someone/something
biased **in favour of/towards** someone/something
biased **reporting/coverage/research/advice**
a biased **opinion/sample/referee/judge**
**heavily** biased

**compelling**
a compelling **argument/reason/testimony**
compelling **data/results/evidence**

**credible**
credible **to** someone
**appear/look/sound** credible
a credible **threat/claim/witness/theory**
**scarcely** credible

**flawed**
a flawed **premise/assumption**
flawed **logic/reasoning**
**fundamentally/seriously/fatally** flawed

**valid**
a valid **reason/point/argument/claim**
a valid **comment/question/comparison/**
  **criticism**
**perfectly/equally/entirely** valid

# Unit 19

## Adjectives describing quantity and degree:
**abundant**
abundant **wildlife/evidence/resources**
an abundant **supply/element**

**marked**

a marked **contrast/improvement/
  increase/difference**
**clearly/most/more** marked

**negligible**

a negligible **impact/effect/contribution**
a negligible **amount/level/risk/cost**
**almost/essentially** negligible

## Adjectives describing degree of certainty:
**definitive**

a definitive **answer/agreement/
  statement/conclusion**
definitive **proof**

**tentative**

a tentative **step/agreement/settlement/deal**
a tentative **conclusion/thesis/theory**

## Adverbs describing quantity and degree:
**marginally**

marginally **profitable/low/high**
**increase/rise/decline/improve** marginally

# The International English Language Testing System (IELTS) Test

IELTS is jointly managed by the British Council, Cambridge ESOL Examinations and IDP Education, Australia.

There are two versions of the test:

- Academic
- General Training

Academic is for students wishing to study at undergraduate or postgraduate levels in an English-medium environment.

General Training is for people who wish to migrate to an English-speaking country.

This book is primarily for students taking the Academic version.

## The Test

There are four modules:

| | |
|---|---|
| **Listening** | 30 minutes, plus 10 minutes for transferring answers to the answer sheet |
| | NB: the audio is heard *only once*. |
| | Approx. 10 questions per section |
| | Section 1: two speakers discuss a social situation |
| | Section 2: one speaker talks about a non-academic topic |
| | Section 3: up to four speakers discuss an educational project |
| | Section 4: one speaker gives a talk of general academic interest |
| **Reading** | 60 minutes |
| | 3 texts, taken from authentic sources, on general, academic topics. They may contain diagrams, charts, etc. |
| | 40 questions: may include multiple choice, sentence completion, completing a diagram, graph or chart, choosing headings, yes/no, true/false questions, classification and matching exercises. |
| **Writing** | Task 1: 20 minutes: description of a table, chart, graph or diagram (150 words minimum) |
| | Task 2: 40 minutes: an essay in response to an argument or problem (250 words minimum) |
| **Speaking** | 11–14 minutes |
| | A three-part face-to-face oral interview with an examiner. |
| | The interview is recorded. |
| | Part 1: introductions and general questions (4–5 mins) |
| | Part 2: individual long turn (3–4 mins) – the candidate is given a task, has one minute to prepare, then talks for 1–2 minutes, with some questions from the examiner. |
| | Part 3: two-way discussion (4–5 mins): the examiner asks further questions on the topic from Part 2, and gives the candidate the opportunity to discuss more abstract issues or ideas. |
| **Timetabling** | Listening, Reading and Writing must be taken on the same day, and in the order listed above. Speaking can be taken up to 7 days before or after the other modules. |
| **Scoring** | Each section is given a band score. The average of the four scores produces the Overall Band Score. You do not pass or fail IELTS; you receive a score. |

## IELTS and the Common European Framework of Reference

The CEFR shows the level of the learner and is used for many English as a Foreign Language examinations. The table below shows the approximate CEFR level and the equivalent IELTS Overall Band Score:

| CEFR description | CEFR code | IELTS Band Score |
|---|---|---|
| Proficient user | C2 | 9 |
| (Advanced) | C1 | 7–8 |
| Independent user | B2 | 5–6.5 |
| (Intermediate – Upper Intermediate) | B1 | 4–5 |

This table contains the general descriptors for the band scores 1–9:

| IELTS Band Scores | | |
|---|---|---|
| 9 | Expert user | Has fully operational command of the language: appropriate, accurate and fluent with complete understanding. |
| 8 | Very good user | Has fully operational command of the language, with only occasional unsystematic inaccuracies and inappropriacies. Misunderstandings may occur in unfamiliar situations. Handles complex detailed argumentation well. |
| 7 | Good user | Has operational command of the language, though with occasional inaccuracies, inappropriacies and misunderstandings in some situations. Generally handles complex language well and understands detailed reasoning. |
| 6 | Competent user | Has generally effective command of the language despite some inaccuracies, inappropriacies and misunderstandings. Can use and understand fairly complex language, particularly in familiar situations. |
| 5 | Modest user | Has partial command of the language, coping with overall meaning in most situations, though is likely to make many mistakes. Should be able to handle basic communication in own field. |
| 4 | Limited user | Basic competence is limited to familiar situations. Has frequent problems in understanding and expression. Is not able to use complex language. |
| 3 | Extremely limited user | Conveys and understands only general meaning in very familiar situations. Frequent breakdowns in communication occur. |
| 2 | Intermittent user | No real communication is possible except for the most basic information using isolated words or short formulae in familiar situations and to meet immediate needs. Has great difficulty understanding spoken and written English. |
| 1 | Non user | Essentially has no ability to use the language beyond possibly a few isolated words. |
| 0 | Did not attempt the test | No assessable information provided. |

## Marking

The Listening and Reading papers have 40 items, each worth one mark if correctly answered. Here are some examples of how marks are translated into band scores:

Listening:
- 16 out of 40 correct answers: band score 5
- 23 out of 40 correct answers: band score 6
- 30 out of 40 correct answers: band score 7

Reading
- 15 out of 40 correct answers: band score 5
- 23 out of 40 correct answers: band score 6
- 30 out of 40 correct answers: band score 7

Writing and Speaking are marked according to performance descriptors.
Writing: examiners award a band score for each of four areas with equal weighting:

- Task achievement (Task 1)
- Task response (Task 2)
- Coherence and cohesion
- Lexical resource and grammatical range and accuracy

Speaking: examiners award a band score for each of four areas with equal weighting:

- Fluency and coherence
- Lexical resource
- Grammatical range
- Accuracy and pronunciation

For full details of how the examination is scored and marked, go to: www.ielts.org